ANOTHER 25 CRIMES THAT ROCKED THE WORLD

MORE DEVASTATING CRIMES THAT CHANGED HISTORY

MATTHEW KELL TAYLOR

INTRODUCTION

Crime has always been a part of human history, but some criminal acts stand out not only for their audacity or brutality, but for the profound impact they have on the public. From high-profile cases that captivated the world's attention to less known but equally consequential events, these crimes have shaped societal attitudes, influenced public policy, and sometimes even changed the course of history. In this eclectic collection, we explore a variety of crimes that, through their nature or aftermath, have left an indelible mark on the collective consciousness.

The crimes presented here are as diverse as the individuals and systems involved, ranging from infamous figures whose criminal acts sparked outrage, to more subtle yet deeply troubling crimes that exposed systemic injustices. Whether it's a criminal act that caused a public outcry, led to widespread societal reform, or served as a reflection of deeper social issues, each event had ripple effects that extended far beyond its immediate victims and perpetrators. These crimes forced society to confront uncomfortable truths, challenge preconceived notions, and, in some cases, demand change.

By examining these varied criminal events, we gain a window into the ways in which crimes can affect not just the lives of those directly involved, but the broader public as well. They challenge our perceptions of justice, morality, and the systems designed to maintain order. Through their stories, we can better understand how crime continues to shape the world around us.

If you enjoy this book check out other titles by this author

50 Crimes That Rocked The World
40 Deadly Women
25 Killer Kids
Kids Who Kill Kids

All available on Amazon as ebook or in print

ABOUT THE AUTHOR

Matthew Kell Taylor is a true crime writer with a passion for uncovering the darkest corners of human nature. Taylor's first book "50 CRIMES THAT ROCKED THE WORLD" was met with critical acclaim, earning him recognition for his meticulous attention to detail and his ability to humanize the victims and perpetrators alike. His second book "40 DEADLY WOMEN" followed the same path.

In his highly anticipated third book, "25 KILLER KIDS" Taylor continues to take readers on a gripping journey into the minds of those who commit the unthinkable—children who kill. Drawing from real-life cases, he expertly navigates the delicate and disturbing topic, exploring the psychological, social, and environmental factors that lead to such horrifying acts. Taylor's unparalleled dedication to understanding the intricacies of criminal behavior shines through, offering both insight and empathy as he explores the disturbing nature of juvenile violence.

Taylor then turns his attention to the unthinkable. In 20 KIDS WHO KILL KIDS and we take another disturbing journey to the very depths of incredible cruelty and depravity, committed by the least likely perpetrators…our own children! Not an easy read but the victims deserve a hearing beyond the court doors.

Now in "ANOTHER 25 CRIMES THAT ROCKED THE WORLD" he returns with an eclectic selection of crimes that had a noted effect on all involved and, because of their notoriety had far reaching effects around the planet.

A skilled storyteller, Matthew Kell Taylor continues to captivate audiences with his in-depth investigations, delivering compelling narratives that are as thought-provoking as they are chilling. His work remains a testament to his commitment to uncovering the truth, no matter how uncomfortable it may be.

For my Family

Disclaimer

The information presented in this book has been researched and compiled to the best of the author's ability using available sources at the time of publication. While every effort has been made to ensure the accuracy and veracity of the facts, the nature of true crime investigation often involves varying accounts, conflicting sources, and evolving details. Some events, dates, or names may differ depending on different interpretations of the evidence and the perspectives of those involved.

The author does not guarantee the absolute accuracy of all the facts presented, as new information may emerge or perspectives may shift after publication. Additionally, the portrayal of individuals, events, or legal proceedings may reflect the interpretation of available sources, rather than definitive or universally accepted truths. Readers are encouraged to seek out additional resources and conduct further research to obtain a fuller understanding of the cases discussed.

This book is intended as a work of non-fiction based on the information available at the time, and it is not meant to serve as an official or legal record.

Copyright © 2025 by Matthew Kell Taylor
All rights reserved.
No part of this book may be reproduced in any form or by any electronic or mechanical means, including information storage and retrieval systems, without written permission from the author, except for the use of brief quotations in a book review.

CONTENTS

1. Harvey Weinstein	1
2. The 2011 Norway attacks	13
3. 7/7 London Bombings	21
4. 9/11 Twin Tower Attacks	30
5. Gambino Crime Cartel	40
6. Manchester Arena Bombing	47
7. The Illegal Adoption Trade	57
8. The Exxon Valdiz Oil Spill	67
9. Jeffrey Epstein	73
10. The 2002 Bali Bombings	83
11. Ashley Madison Website Hack	93
12. The Darfur Genocide	100
13. Martha Stewart Insider Trading Scandal	107
14. The #Me Too Movement	115
15. The Trafficking Of Human Organs	122
16. The Holocaust	129
17. The Disappearance of flight MH370	140
18. The 2014 JP Morgan Chase Bank Hacking	147
19. The Cocaine Trade	155
20. The Boston Marathon Bombing	163
21. The Moscow Theater Hostage Crisis	169
22. The Sex Grooming Gangs in The UK	175
23. The My Lai Massacre	185
24. The Bhopal Disaster	194
25. The Madrid Train Bombings	201

CHAPTER 1
HARVEY WEINSTEIN
DISGRACEFUL ABUSE OF POWER

Harvey Weinstein

Harvey Weinstein was once a towering figure in Hollywood, a man whose name was synonymous with power, influence, and success in the entertainment industry. As a co-founder of Miramax Films and later The Weinstein Company, Weinstein had shaped the careers of some of the most significant names in cinema. Yet, behind the glitz and glamour, his name would soon be associated with something far darker—allegations of sexual abuse, harassment, and coercion that would reverberate across the globe, leading to his eventual fall from grace.

HARVEY WEINSTEIN'S RISE TO POWER

Harvey Weinstein's ascent to the pinnacle of Hollywood power is a story of ambition, manipulation, and an unrelenting drive to control the entertainment industry. He was born in 1952 in Queens, New York, to a middle-class Jewish family. His father, Max Weinstein, was a diamond cutter, and his mother, Miriam, was a teacher. From a young age, Weinstein exhibited the kind of confidence and ambition that would later define his career, but it wasn't the kind of ambition that would endear him to everyone in his life.

Weinstein's early years were far from glamorous, yet his future in show business would be anything but ordinary. After graduating from the University of Buffalo in 1973, Weinstein moved to New York City, where he and his brother Bob Weinstein initially worked in the music business. The brothers co-founded a small independent concert promotion company, which eventually led them to start a company called Miramax Films in 1979.

The name "Miramax" was taken from their parents: Miriam and Max. What began as a small independent film production company soon turned into a powerhouse in the film industry, largely due to Harvey's ferocity and unparalleled drive. While Bob managed much of the company's business affairs, it was Harvey who would emerge as the dominant force behind Miramax, steering the company through a series of successful acquisitions, negotiations, and bold filmmaking decisions.

THE BIRTH OF MIRAMAX FILMS

In the early days of Miramax, Harvey's hunger for success was evident in his tireless work ethic and his ability to recognize and seize opportunities in an ever-evolving market. What separated Weinstein from other film producers was his ability to mix artistic sensibility with a ruthless business sense. Miramax Films became known for releasing edgy, independent films that were both critically acclaimed and commercially successful. Harvey's ability to bring fresh, original films to the forefront of the entertainment industry was his calling card.

One of Weinstein's first major successes came in 1988 when Miramax distributed *Sex, Lies, and Videotape*, a film by Steven Soderbergh that had a modest budget but went on to become a breakout hit. The film was both a box office success and a critical darling, winning the Palme d'Or at the Cannes Film Festival. For Weinstein, the film marked a pivotal moment in his career. It proved that independent films could succeed in the Hollywood marketplace, and it was just the beginning of what would be a series of ground-breaking films.

Despite the success of *Sex, Lies, and Videotape*, it was the 1990s that truly solidified Harvey Weinstein's reputation as one of the most powerful figures in Hollywood. Weinstein, a man who was always at the intersection of business and creativity, built an empire by doing what many in Hollywood thought was impossible—making low-budget, independent films into high-profile, Oscar-winning fare. Miramax, under his leadership, became the gold standard for independent cinema.

THE HOLLYWOOD MOGUL EMERGES

By the mid-1990s, Weinstein had built Miramax into one of the most influential independent film studios in the world. His vision was clear: he was going to dominate the Oscars and put independent film on the map. Miramax was responsible for a string of high-profile films that garnered critical acclaim and awards attention. This included Quentin Tarantino's *Pulp Fiction* (1994), a film that not only redefined independent cinema but also changed the landscape of Hollywood filmmaking itself. Weinstein's aggressive marketing tactics and his ability to get films seen by the right people were key to the success of *Pulp Fiction* at the Academy Awards, where it won several nominations, including Best Picture.

Another landmark moment came in 1997, when *The English Patient*—a period drama directed by Anthony Minghella—won nine Academy Awards, including Best Picture and Best Director. The success of *The English Patient* cemented Miramax's place in the Hollywood elite and demonstrated Harvey's power to make films that both appealed to a broad audience and captivated the Academy voters. During this period, Weinstein's reputation as a ruthless and highly effective producer was solidified, and he became a key player in the world of Oscar campaigns.

Yet, it wasn't just his ability to select scripts and market films that propelled Weinstein to the top. He also used a unique combination of charm, intimidation, and manipulation to ensure that the studio's films received the attention they deserved. Weinstein, a notoriously difficult and volatile individual, became infamous for his aggressive tactics, bullying directors, and pressuring journalists to cover his films favorably. Many in Hollywood feared him, and the power he wielded was unmatched.

Miramax's influence continued to grow throughout the 1990s, producing films such as *Shakespeare in Love* (1998), which won seven Oscars, including Best Picture, and was a commercial success. The film, which was a romantic period drama set in Elizabethan England, was one of the most successful films of the decade, and it further entrenched Weinstein's reputation as a master of the Oscar race.

THE EXPANSION TO THE WEINSTEIN COMPANY

By the early 2000s, the Weinstein brothers' relationship with the Walt Disney Company, which had acquired Miramax in 1993, began to sour. The Weinsteins were frustrated with Disney's increasing control over the studio's operations, particularly in terms of the types of films that were being made. In 2005, Harvey and Bob Weinstein left Miramax and founded The Weinstein Company, a new film studio designed to give them full control over their productions.

With The Weinstein Company, Harvey continued to operate as the face of the brand, expanding beyond the realms of film production and distribution into television and even Broadway. His aggressive tactics in securing distribution rights to major films like *The King's Speech* (2010) and *The Artist* (2011) solidified his position as a major force in Hollywood. Weinstein's knack for recognizing potential Oscar contenders continued to keep him at the forefront of the entertainment industry, and The Weinstein Company quickly became a contender for Best Picture nominations and wins.

However, by this point, Weinstein's darker reputation had also started to follow him. Behind his power and success, there were growing whispers of sexual harassment and inappropriate behavior. Many women in the industry began to feel the repercussions of Weinstein's dual role as both a Hollywood kingmaker and a manipulator of those seeking work. Those who worked with him were often subjected to pressure, intimidation, and unwanted advances, and his penchant for using his power to control those around him would soon be revealed in full.

THE MAKING OF A HOLLYWOOD TITAN

Through sheer force of will, Harvey Weinstein crafted a lasting legacy in Hollywood. His rise to power was built on his ability to recognize talent, broker deals, and bend the rules of the industry to his advantage. His relentless ambition and drive were central to his success, but they also formed the basis for his manipulative, abusive behavior. Weinstein's influence, at its peak, stretched far beyond the walls of Miramax and The Weinstein Company—he was a fixture at the Academy Awards, a gatekeeper for young talent, and a feared figure in the world of filmmaking.

But as the decades wore on, Harvey Weinstein's dark secrets would slowly begin to surface, forever tarnishing the legacy of a man who had once been seen as a symbol of Hollywood success.

THE CULTURE OF FEAR

As one of Hollywood's most influential figures, Weinstein wielded significant power over those who sought to make it in the film industry. He often operated behind closed doors, where his reputation as a "kingmaker" was bolstered by his ability to launch the careers of aspiring actresses and filmmakers. Yet, as many soon discovered, this power came at a horrific price.

For decades, whispers of Weinstein's lecherous behavior circulated throughout Hollywood. He was known for using his position to coerce women into sexual acts, leveraging promises of film roles or career advancement in exchange for sexual favors. Weinstein's modus operandi was insidious: he would often invite women to private meetings, sometimes under the guise of discussing career opportunities, only to later demand sexual favors. If his advances were rejected, the consequences were swift and severe—promising careers were suddenly derailed, and women were blacklisted from future opportunities.

The power imbalance was immense. Young actresses and aspiring stars, eager for a chance to make it in an industry known for its cutthroat nature, found themselves in compromising situations. Weinstein, who had a reputation for being ruthless, used his authority to manipulate, intimidate, and control these women. For many, the fear of losing their careers or being ostracized by the industry was enough to silence them.

But over time, these whispers would grow louder and take on the form of public accusations. The culture of silence that allowed Weinstein's abuse to continue for so long was finally beginning to crack.

THE ACCUSATIONS AGAINST HARVEY WEINSTEIN

Harvey Weinstein, once a towering figure in Hollywood, had it all—the power to launch careers, shape films, and hold the keys to the industry's most coveted opportunities. But behind his public persona as a mogul, a culture of fear, manipulation, and exploitation existed that would ultimately unravel his career and expose a deeply disturbing pattern of abuse. Weinstein's fall from grace, triggered by multiple sexual harassment and assault accusations, would reverberate not just through Hollywood but across industries worldwide, igniting a cultural reckoning and the #MeToo movement.

THE EARLY WHISPERS OF MISCONDUCT

For decades, rumors swirled around Weinstein's behavior. Those who worked with him—especially young women—knew the cost of ambition in Hollywood could be high. In private conversations, many actors, assistants, and filmmakers shared stories of Weinstein's inappropriate behavior: the promise of film roles in exchange for sexual favors, the offers to "help" actresses in their careers after sexual encounters, and the tales of humiliation, coercion, and manipulation. However, Weinstein's power made him untouchable for a long time. His influence over the careers of both established and aspiring stars, as well as his connections to influential people in the film industry, protected him from serious consequences for years.

Despite the whispers, few dared to speak out publicly. Many believed that doing so would end their careers or lead to immediate blacklisting within the industry. But over time, as more and more women began to recognize that they were not alone, the silence started to break.

THE NEW YORK TIMES INVESTIGATION

In October 2017, a *New York Times* investigation, led by reporters Jodi Kantor and Megan Twohey, finally brought Weinstein's alleged abuses to light. The article featured the testimonies of several women who accused Weinstein of harassment and assault, including actresses Ashley Judd and Rose McGowan. Their stories, along with those of others, detailed how Weinstein would frequently use his power as a producer to lure women into private meetings, only to proposition them sexually or attempt to coerce them into sexual acts.

Ashley Judd, one of the first actresses to speak out publicly, revealed that Weinstein had made unwelcome advances toward her during a meeting in the late 1990s. The encounter took place at a hotel room, where Weinstein allegedly greeted Judd in a bathrobe and asked her to massage him. When Judd rejected his advances, she felt both threatened and humiliated. While she was able to escape the encounter without further harassment, the experience left her deeply scarred.

Similarly, actress Rose McGowan, known for her role in *Scream* and *Charmed*, came forward with a harrowing account of sexual assault. McGowan claimed that in 1997, when she was just 23, Weinstein sexually assaulted her in a hotel room at the Sundance Film Festival. McGowan's accusation was particularly significant because she had previously reached a settlement with Weinstein in exchange for her silence. However, the *New York Times* report gave her the courage to break that silence.

THE NEW YORKER EXPOSÉ

Just days after *The New York Times* published its report, *The New Yorker* followed suit with an extensive investigation by Ronan Farrow, which uncovered additional victims and more shocking details about Weinstein's predatory behavior. The report featured allegations of sexual assault and rape from multiple women, including actress Asia Argento, who had long been vocal about her experiences with Weinstein. Argento claimed that Weinstein raped her in 1997 when she was 21 years old, during a meeting at the Cannes Film Festival. She recalled that Weinstein made sexual advances, and when she rejected him, he became violent. Argento, like many others, had kept the experience private for years out of fear of professional retaliation and public shaming.

Farrow's investigation also revealed how Weinstein used his position to suppress any accusations against him. Many women had signed non-disclosure agreements (NDAs) as part of settlements, which legally prevented them from speaking out. This was a common tactic Weinstein employed to avoid exposure. He also used his influence to bully reporters and other

Hollywood professionals into keeping quiet about the allegations. In one particularly disturbing example, Weinstein allegedly hired private investigators to gather dirt on his accusers and journalists pursuing stories about him.

The *New Yorker* article included testimony from several women who recounted similar experiences. Their stories painted a picture of a man who manipulated women through promises of career advancement, only to turn their dreams into nightmares once they were isolated in a hotel room or private meeting. His pattern of behavior, repeated with impunity over decades, became undeniable.

THE SCOPE OF WEINSTEIN'S ABUSE

As more women came forward, the scale of Weinstein's abuses became apparent. Some of his victims were famous actresses, while others were aspiring professionals or lesser-known figures within the entertainment industry. Some women spoke about harassment that took place during private meetings, while others described outright sexual assault. What remained consistent across the stories, however, was Weinstein's abuse of power, and his ability to evade consequences due to his status as a powerful Hollywood producer.

Actress Gwyneth Paltrow, one of Weinstein's early protégées, also came forward with her own disturbing experience. Paltrow revealed that in the 1990s, when she was just 22 years old and working on the film *Emma*, Weinstein had made advances on her. She was reportedly summoned to his hotel room, where he placed his hands on her and suggested they go to the bedroom. Paltrow, like many others, felt trapped. She eventually confided in her boyfriend, Brad Pitt, who confronted Weinstein and allegedly threatened him.

Other women, including actresses like Mira Sorvino and Angelina Jolie, also spoke out, recounting similar incidents of harassment. Sorvino, for example, described how Weinstein made sexual advances toward her when they were working together on the film *Mimic*. After she rejected him, her career stalled, and she claimed that Weinstein's influence led to her being blacklisted from Hollywood. Jolie recounted how Weinstein tried to sexually harass her while she was working on *Playing by Heart* in the late 1990s, and she later told her agent to make sure she never worked with him again.

The wave of accusations against Weinstein eventually grew to include more than 80 women, spanning multiple continents and decades. Many women had long feared that speaking out would cost them their careers, but the collective power of the *New York Times* and *The New Yorker* investigations gave them the platform and support they needed to break their silence.

THE IMPACT OF THE ACCUSATIONS

The public revelation of Weinstein's abuses had far-reaching consequences. Not only did it lead to the end of his career, but it also ignited the #MeToo movement, which encouraged women across industries to share their own stories of sexual harassment and assault. The hashtag became a rallying cry for those who had suffered in silence, and it gave voice to the countless women who had experienced similar abuse but had never been able to speak out.

Weinstein's behavior, once dismissed or ignored, was now the subject of intense scrutiny, and his public downfall sent a shockwave through Hollywood and beyond. Powerful men who had long been able to avoid accountability now found themselves under investigation or facing public backlash. The #MeToo movement reshaped the way society viewed sexual harassment, and it led to an increased focus on the need for systemic change in how such allegations are handled.

LEGAL AND CRIMINAL CONSEQUENCES

The New York County District Attorneys Office charged Weinstein with "rape, criminal sex act, sex abuse and sexual misconduct for incidents involving two separate women" on May 25, 2018. He was arrested the same day after surrendering to the New York City Police Department, NYPD) and released after US$1 million bail was posted on his behalf. He surrendered his passport and was required to wear an ankle monitor, with travel being restricted to New York and Connecticut. His lawyer Benjamin Brafman, said Weinstein would plead not guilty. A trial date was set for January 6, 2020. On that date, Weinstein was also charged in Los Angeles with raping one woman and sexually assaulting another in 2013.

After deliberating for five days, a jury convicted Weinstein on February

24, 2020, of two of five criminal charges: one count of criminal sexual assault in the first degree and one count of rape in the third degree. The jury found him not guilty regarding predatory sexual assault, which could have led to a life sentence. Weinstein was remanded to jail at Rikers Island in New York City pending his sentencing hearing on March 11, when he was sentenced to 23 years in prison. Weinstein was then transferred to Wende Correctional Facility in Erie County, New York. Through his attorneys, Weinstein stated that he would appeal the verdict. Weinstein was stripped of his honorary (Commander of the Most Excellent Order of the British Empire) on September 18, 2020. Once incarcerated, Weinstein hired prison consultant Craig Rothfeld. By June 2021, Weinstein had been transferred to the Mohawk Correctional facility in Rome New York.

On June 2, 2022, the New York State Supreme Court, Appellate Division, First Department upheld the verdicts and judgment on appeal. For the court's decision, Judge Angela Mazzarelli wrote, "We perceive no basis for reducing the sentence, and we have considered defendant's remaining arguments and find them unavailing." On August 25, 2022, Weinstein was granted a further appeal before the New York Court of Appeals.

CALIFORNIA CONVICTION

On July 20, 2021, Weinstein was flown to Los Angeles and taken to the Twin Towers Correctional Facility. The trial in Los Angeles commenced in October 2022. Weinstein was charged with 11 counts of rape, forcible oral copulation and sexual battery, stemming from alleged acts between 2004 and 2013. He was found guilty of three of seven charges (four of the initial 11 charges were dropped) on December 19, 2022. Convictions included charges of rape, forced oral copulation and third-degree sexual misconduct. On February 23, 2023, Weinstein was sentenced to 16 years in prison for these convictions. His sentence in California prisons must be served separately from (i.e., consecutively to rather than concurrently to) his time served in New York. Weinstein is appealing the Los Angeles conviction. On April 11, 2023, Weinstein was extradited from California and back to upstate New York's the Mohawk Correctional Facility. After the New York convictions were overturned in April 2024, and plans were made to retry him in New York City, Weinstein was transferred back to Riker's Island prison.

On June 8, 2022, Weinstein was formally charged by the Metropolitan Police with two counts of indecent assault against a woman in London between July 31 and August 31, 1996.

On July 9, 2024, New York prosecutors announced an investigation was underway for additional claims against Weinstein for sexual assault, including for claims that fall within the state's statute of limitations, though no indictment was immediately sent to the grand jury.

NEW YORK CONVICTION OVERTURNED

On April 25, 2024, the New York Court of Appeals overturned the New York rape convictions and said that the trial judge had made "egregious errors" with the attorney stating Weinstein had been "tried on his character, not the evidence." The Court of Appeals ordered a retrial.

After the New York appeal ruling, a number of actresses who had made allegations against Weinstein responded:

Ashley Judd, who was among the first to disclose her rape, told the *New York Times*: "That is unfair to survivors. We still live in our truth. And we know what happened." Later at a press conference, Judd added: "This is what it's like to be a woman in America, living with male entitlement to our bodies."

Roseanna Arquette, who disclosed that Weinstein assaulted her, said in a statement to the *Hollywood Reporter*: "Harvey was rightfully convicted. It's unfortunate that the court has overturned his conviction. As a survivor, I am beyond disappointed."

Rose McGowan, who also shared her story of assault from Weinstein, said in a video statement: "No matter what they overturn, they cannot take away who we are and what we know, what we've gone through and what we can achieve in this life. We are not victims. We are people that were injured by evil."

RETRIAL

Despite the successful appeal, Weinstein remains set to face a retrial for the overturned New York convictions in the fall of 2024. During a court hearing on July 19, 2024, Judge Curtis Farber ruled that Weinstein would be retried and tentatively set for the retrial to start on November 12, 2024. Despite this, Farber also ruled that previous plans to have the retrial start in September 2024 were still an option, and the start date of the retrial would depend on pretrial discoveries. Weinstein's lawyers have called for the retrial to begin as soon as possible. On January 29, 2025, Judge Farber set the retrial to date to April 15, 2025.

ADDITIONAL CHARGES IN NEW YORK

On September 12, 2024, a New York grand jury indicted Weinstein on new charges, as announced by prosecutors from the Manhattan District Attorney's office. The specific charges remain unknown, as the indictment is sealed and will be revealed during Weinstein's arraignment. On September 18, 2024, Weinstein was arraigned in New York for this new indictment, entering a plea of not guilty to one count of criminal sexual act in the first degree. The prosecution filed a motion to consolidate the new charges into Weinstein's retrial rather than have two separate New York trials. The presiding judge granted the prosecution's motion to consolidate on October 23.

THE AFTERMATH OF HARVEY WEINSTEIN'S FALL

Harvey Weinstein's downfall marked a seismic shift in the entertainment industry and beyond, forever altering the dynamics of power, gender, and accountability. Once a celebrated Hollywood mogul, Weinstein's career came to an abrupt and catastrophic end after dozens of women accused him of sexual harassment, assault, and rape. These revelations not only destroyed Weinstein's empire but also ignited a global movement for justice and equality—one that would force industries worldwide to confront their complicity in systemic abuse. The aftermath of Weinstein's exposure has been felt across every facet of society, from the entertainment industry to politics, business, and beyond.

CHAPTER 2
THE 2011 NORWAY ATTACKS
SLAUGHTER IN UTOYA, NORWAY

Anders Behring Breivik

On July 22, 2011, Norway was rocked by a series of attacks that shocked not only the nation but also the world. What began as a calculated and violent strike in Oslo's government district soon escalated into a horrific massacre on the island of Utøya. The attacks, carried out by Anders Behring Breivik, left 77 people dead—most of them teenagers—and many others injured. It was a day that would forever change Norway, leading to deep reflections on the causes of far-right extremism, the challenges of preventing terrorism, and the values that the country holds dear.

This account of the events leading to and following the 2011 Norway attacks will explore Breivik's motivations, the execution of his attacks, the aftermath, and the lasting impact on Norwegian society.

BREIVIK'S RADICALIZATION

Breivik's radicalization did not occur overnight. Born in Oslo on February 13, 1979, he was raised by his mother, as his father had largely disappeared from his life. Breivik's early years were relatively uneventful, and he appeared to lead a fairly ordinary life. However, as he matured, he became increasingly disillusioned with what he saw as the deterioration of European culture and values. His radicalization was shaped by his growing obsession with anti-Islamic ideology, a fear of the so-called "Islamization" of Europe, and a deep disdain for the political left.

By the mid-2000s, Breivik began to immerse himself in extreme far-right literature. He was particularly influenced by figures like Robert Spencer and Geert Wilders, who were vocal in their opposition to Islamic immigration. Breivik's views became more extreme over time, and he started to develop the belief that Europe was under siege from both Islamic immigrants and left-wing politicians, whom he blamed for enabling the spread of Islam through lax immigration policies.

Breivik also became convinced that the Labour Party in Norway, led by Prime Minister Jens Stoltenberg at the time, was part of the problem. He felt that the party's liberal stance on immigration and its support for multiculturalism had undermined the social fabric of Norwegian society and allowed Muslim immigrants to gain a foothold in Europe.

In 2010, Breivik began planning the attacks. He meticulously crafted a plan that would allow him to strike a blow against what he considered the forces of multiculturalism. His goal was to kill as many of those associated with the Labour Party as possible and to send a strong message to the world about the dangers of unchecked immigration.

THE MANIFESTO

Before carrying out his attacks, Breivik posted a 1,500-page manifesto online. This document, titled *2083: A European Declaration of Independence*, outlined his deeply anti-Islamic and anti-left-wing ideology. In it, Breivik portrayed himself as a defender of European culture, lamenting the rise of multiculturalism and the decline of traditional Christian values in Europe. He referred to his attacks as a "necessary" act to stop the ongoing erosion of European identity.

The manifesto also contained detailed accounts of Breivik's planning process. He described his weaponry, his training regimen, and his ideological motivations. The manifesto was not just a call to arms for like-minded individuals, but also a justification for the horrific actions he was about to take. Breivik believed that his actions would inspire others to rise up and start a "crusade" against Islam and the political left. His hope was that his attacks would spark a larger civil war in Europe, leading to the purging of Muslim immigrants and the political left from the continent.

Breivik's manifesto also contained a detailed analysis of the perceived dangers posed by Islamic immigration. He argued that the growing number of Muslims in Europe would eventually lead to the collapse of European culture and civilization. This idea of a looming demographic crisis was central to Breivik's thinking and was one of the driving forces behind his decision to carry out such a violent and dramatic act of terror.

THE OSLO BOMBING

Breivik's attacks were methodical and well-planned. The first phase of his plan unfolded in Oslo, the capital of Norway. At 15:25 (3:25 PM) on July 22, 2011, Breivik detonated a powerful bomb outside the government quarter of Oslo. The bomb, placed inside a car, exploded with a devastating force. The blast ripped through the streets, shattering windows, tearing apart buildings, and sending debris flying through the air.

Eight people were killed in the explosion; the blast, shock wave and debris immediately killed six people, while two others died quickly afterwards from their wounds. Of the 325 people estimated to have been in the government buildings, around them and in the surrounding area, at least 209 people received physical injuries from the blast and debris. While most were relatively minor and could be treated at the local casualty clinic, 12 people received more serious injuries. Ten were sent to hospital Ulleval University Hospital, four with moderate to serious and six with critical injuries, and two to Aker University Hospital. A doctor at one of the Oslo University Hospital said the hospital staff were treating head, chest and abdominal wounds.

Prime Minister Jens Stoltenberg was at his official residence near the Royal Palace, preparing the speech he was scheduled to give at Utøya the next day. Norway's finance minister Sigbjorn Johnsen, was on vacation in Denmark at the time.

Fewer people than usual were in the area because the bombing took place during July, the usual holiday month for Norwegians, and since it was Friday afternoon, most government employees had gone home for the weekend.

FATALITIES IN OSLO

- Tove Ashill Knutsen, 56, Oslo
  - Hanna Endresen, 61, Oslo
  - Kai Hauge, 32, Oslo
  - Jon Vegard Lervag, 32, Oslo
  - Ida Marie Hill, 34, Oslo
  - Hanne Ekroll Loevlie, 30, Oslo
  - Anne Lise Holter, 51, Valer i Oestfold, Oestfold county
  - Kjersti Berg Sand, 26, Nord-Ordal

While the bombing itself was horrific, it was only a prelude to the far greater horror that would unfold on Utøya Island, 40 kilometers (about 25 miles) away. Breivik had timed the bombing to draw attention away from his second, more deadly attack. His goal was to create confusion and distraction, allowing him to carry out the massacre without interference.

THE UTØYA MASSACRE

After the bombing, Breivik drove to a ferry terminal in Oslo, where he boarded a boat that would take him to Utøya Island. Utøya was the site of the annual summer camp for the Workers' Youth League (AUF), a political youth organization affiliated with the Labour Party. The camp hosted about 600 young people, aged 14 to 25, many of whom were participating in discussions on politics and social issues, as well as engaging in recreational activities.

Upon arriving at the island at approximately 17:00 (5:00 PM), Breivik began his massacre. Dressed in a police uniform, he initially fooled many of the camp's attendees into thinking he was a police officer sent to investigate the bombing in Oslo. As he moved through the camp, he began shooting his victims. Many of the young people tried to flee, while others sought refuge in the water, swimming to nearby boats or to the mainland.

The scope of what happened at the island was initially very confusing, and the first official figures given was that at least 10 people had been killed. As the evening progressed several eyewitness reports put this number in doubt, and at approximately 03:50 (CEST) on 23 July, NRK1 and TV2 the two primary Norwegian television networks, broadcast a live press conference from the "Sentrum politistasjon" in Oslo where Norway's National Police Commissioner Oystein Marland stated the number of fatalities at Utøya to have reached "at least 80" with the count expected to increase.

On 25 July, a police spokesperson revealed that the death toll of the victims on Utøya had been revised downwards to 68 after the casualties had been counted on their return to the mainland. They added that the number of people missing was still high and that the number of casualties could be as high as 86. On 29 July police announced that one of the severely wounded victims from Utøya had died in hospital, bringing the death toll from the island massacre to 69.

On 26 July, the Norwegian police began releasing the names and dates of birth of the victims on their website. By 29 July, the names of all 77 victims (8 from the bomb attack, 69 from Utøya) had been published, the last, a shooting victim, having been found on the 28th.

Of the 69 people who died at the attack on the island, 57 were killed by one or more shots through the head. In total, 67 people were killed by gunshots, 1 died falling from a cliff trying to escape, and 1 drowned trying to swim away from the island. In total, Breivik fired at least 186 shots and still had a "considerable amount of ammunition" left.

In the aftermath, of the 564 people on the island at the time, 69 people died and at least 110 people had received various physical injuries. An estimated 50 people were treated at the locally set up casualty clinic, and were treated for relatively minor injuries such as cuts, bruises and hypothermia after fleeing and swimming from the island. It was cloudy and rainy on Utøya that day, air temperature was varying between 14–15 °C (57–59 °F), water temperature around the island was 14–15°C (57–59 °F) and the shortest distance to the mainland was around 600 metres. Sixty people were transported to surrounding hospitals, 55 with serious to critical injuries. The chief surgeon who treated the wounds at one of the hospitals said he had never seen similar wounds during his 23 years of practice, and explained that the bullets were extremely fragmented in their path through the body. Thirty-three people had been directly hit by one or more bullets and survived, but a

23-year-old man who was shot died two days later in hospital from the bullet wounds to his head and back.

The 564 people on the island at the time were from all over Norway as well as some visitors from foreign countries. The people who died were from 18 of Norway's 19 counties and also a woman from Georgia. Wounded people were from the entire country, including Svalbard, and together with the casualties from Oslo, an average of a quarter of Norway's population knew a victim affected by the attacks, according to a survey done. Several of the dead and wounded, or their parents, were personal friends of high-ranking government ministers. Trond Berntsen, an off-duty, unarmed police officer and step-brother of Norway's crown princess Mette Marit was the first to be shot dead.

The shooting spree lasted for over an hour. Breivik methodically hunted down his victims, targeting those he believed were responsible for spreading left-wing ideologies. His weapon of choice was a Ruger Mini-14 semi-automatic rifle, which he used with deadly precision. Breivik also carried a handgun, though he primarily used the rifle to carry out the killings.

Some victims managed to escape, while others hid or played dead in an attempt to survive. The scene was one of utter chaos, with panicked screams, gunfire, and the sound of waves crashing against the shore. The police, initially unaware of the scale of the attack, were slow to respond. While emergency services began to mobilize, Breivik continued his killing spree without interference.

At 18:30 (6:30 PM), the police finally arrived on the island. Breivik surrendered without resistance, and he was arrested and taken into custody. By the time the massacre ended, 69 people had been killed, most of them teenagers. Many of the victims were shot multiple times, and some were left severely wounded. The youngest victim was just 14 years old.

The Utøya Island massacre became the deadliest mass shooting in Norwegian history, and the shock of such an attack—especially one targeting young people—was felt deeply by the nation. Norway had long prided itself on being a peaceful, open society, and the attack shattered that sense of security.

THE INVESTIGATION AND ARREST

Breivik's arrest was swift, but the investigation into the full extent of the attacks was more complex. Authorities soon learned that the bombing in Oslo and the shooting spree on Utøya were part of a coordinated plan carried out by a single individual. Breivik was charged with multiple counts of murder, attempted murder, and terrorism.

Throughout his interrogation, Breivik showed no remorse for his actions. He defended his decision to carry out the attacks as a necessary step in the fight to protect European civilization from the threat of Islamization. Breivik also expressed a belief that his actions would inspire others to join his cause, though he appeared to have underestimated the global condemnation that followed the attacks.

Breivik's trial began in 2012 and drew widespread attention. Throughout the proceedings, he displayed little emotion, and he continued to argue that his actions were justified. His behavior led some to question his mental state. Experts debated whether he was sane at the time of the attacks. Eventually, the court ruled that Breivik was not suffering from schizophrenia, but he was deemed to be criminally insane. He was sentenced to 21 years in prison, which can be extended indefinitely as long as he is considered a danger to society.

THE AFTERMATH AND NATIONAL RESPONSE

In the aftermath of the attacks, Norway found itself grappling with profound grief. The nation was in mourning for the victims, many of whom were young and had been politically active. The attacks also raised difficult questions about the nature of terrorism, the rise of far-right extremism, and how to prevent such events in the future.

Despite the horror of the attacks, Norway responded with remarkable resilience. Prime Minister Jens Stoltenberg, in particular, emphasized that the attacks would not change the core values of Norwegian society. He called for unity and expressed his commitment to preserving Norway's open, tolerant, and democratic culture. "We are a small country," he said, "but we are strong. We will not let fear divide us."

Stoltenberg's remarks were echoed by citizens across the country, who participated in memorials and vigils for the victims. The attack brought people together in a way that few other events could have. Thousands of Norwegians turned out in support of the survivors and the families of the victims.

Internationally, the attacks were condemned as an assault on European values of democracy and tolerance. World leaders from all political backgrounds expressed their shock and sympathy for Norway. The attacks also prompted renewed discussions about the dangers of far-right extremism and the need for increased vigilance against terrorism.

THE LEGACY OF THE ATTACKS

The 2011 Norway attacks left a permanent mark on the country. Politically, they prompted discussions about immigration policy, the role of the political left, and the need to safeguard against radicalization. In the years following the attacks, Norway has made efforts to bolster its security and counter the rise of extremist ideologies, though it has also remained committed to its democratic principles.

The families of the victims, as well as the survivors, have shown incredible resilience in the years since the attacks. Many have worked to promote peace and tolerance, ensuring that the tragedy is not forgotten and that the lessons learned continue to shape Norway's future.

Ultimately, the 2011 Norway attacks were a horrifying reminder of the capacity for violence in the name of ideology. While Breivik's vision of a divided and fear-stricken Europe failed, the attacks served as a wake-up call to the dangers of far-right extremism and the need to protect the values of democracy, freedom, and unity.

CHAPTER 3
7/7 LONDON BOMBINGS
MASSACRE IN THE CITY

City Under Attack

A CITY SHAKEN

On the morning of July 7, 2005, London, a city that prided itself on its diversity, its public transportation system, and its reputation for resilience, was violently shaken. Four coordinated suicide bombings targeted London's public transport system during the morning rush hour. The attacks resulted in 52 deaths and over 700 injuries, making it one of the deadliest acts of terrorism in British history. The victims came from a wide range of backgrounds: workers, tourists, students, and commuters, all caught in a carefully planned plot that shattered the city's sense of security.

The bombings, later known as the 7/7 bombings, were a direct assault on the values of freedom and tolerance that Britain held dear. The events sent shockwaves across the world, not just for the devastation they caused, but for the realization that British-born individuals were responsible for the carnage. This chapter will examine the timeline of the bombings, the identity and motives of the perpetrators, the immediate aftermath, the investigation, and the broader impact on British society.

THE BUILD-UP: THE RADICALIZATION OF THE BOMBERS

The four men who carried out the 7/7 bombings were British citizens, all of whom had grown up in the United Kingdom. Their radicalization, however, was fueled by a combination of religious extremism, ideological influences, and a sense of alienation from mainstream British society. Their backgrounds, while seemingly ordinary, masked a growing disenchantment with their lives in Britain, which in part led them to embrace the jihadist cause.

Mohammad Sidique Khan

The ringleader of the bombers, Mohammad Sidique Khan, was 30 years old at the time of the attacks. Born in Bradford, England, to Pakistani parents, Khan was an ordinary man who, on the surface, led an unremarkable life. He had worked as a teaching assistant and lived in the Beeston area of Leeds with his wife and child. Despite his outwardly calm demeanor, Khan had become radicalized in the years leading up to the attacks.

Khan's radicalization was primarily influenced by his views on Western foreign policy, especially Britain's involvement in the wars in Iraq and Afghanistan. He was reportedly angered by the death of Muslims in these conflicts and believed that the West was waging a war against Islam. Khan's personal transformation took place gradually, but in the years before the attack, he had embraced an extremist interpretation of Islam. He traveled to Pakistan, where he is believed to have met with extremist figures. It was there, in the months leading up to 7/7, that Khan and his co-conspirators finalized their plan.

Shehzad Tanweer

Shehzad Tanweer, 22, was a second bomber and a close associate of Khan. Tanweer had grown up in Leeds, where he was well-known as a talented cricketer. In his early years, he appeared to be a model student and an active member of his local community. However, in his later teenage years, Tanweer began to distance himself from his family's traditional values and embrace a radical interpretation of Islam.

Tanweer had traveled to Pakistan, where it is believed he became further influenced by radical ideologies. By the time of the 7/7 attacks, Tanweer had completely rejected British society. His anger was directed primarily at what he perceived as the oppression of Muslims by Western powers. He was the mastermind behind the attack on the Aldgate train, where the first explosion occurred. Tanweer's involvement in the bombing would mark the end of his previous life, as he became fully committed to the terrorist cause.

Hasib Hussain

Hasib Hussain, the youngest bomber at just 18 years old, came from a working-class family in Leeds. Hussain was born in the UK to Pakistani parents, and like his co-conspirators, he began to distance himself from mainstream society in the years leading up to the attacks. Hussain's radicalization was primarily a product of internet propaganda and his exposure to extremist ideologies. He had no criminal history, and his background suggested a normal teenage life, but he had become consumed with anger over perceived injustices against Muslims.

Hussain's role in the bombings was to carry out the attack on the bus, which resulted in 13 deaths. The explosion on the number 30 bus in Tavistock Square was the final of the four planned attacks, and it was particularly tragic due to the number of innocent bystanders who lost their lives in what was supposed to be a routine commute.

Germaine Lindsay

Germaine Lindsay, the fourth bomber, was 19 years old at the time of the attack. Lindsay, originally from Jamaica, had converted to Islam in his late teens. While he was born in the Caribbean, Lindsay had lived in the UK for several years and had become a part of the local community in Aylesbury, Buckinghamshire. Like the other bombers, Lindsay's radicalization was gradual and largely influenced by his growing resentment of Western foreign policy and his search for a cause to belong to.

Lindsay's role in the bombing was to detonate an explosive device on a train traveling between King's Cross and Russell Square. This explosion was one of the deadliest, killing 26 people, including Lindsay himself.

THE ATTACK: A DAY OF TERROR

The 7/7 London bombings, one of the most devastating terrorist attacks in British history, left 52 innocent people dead and more than 700 injured. These victims, from all walks of life, were caught in an unspeakable act of violence that forever altered their families, their communities, and the very fabric of London itself. This chapter will focus on the victims of the 7/7 bombings, the impact on their families and friends, and the lasting legacy of their lives.

The Victims of the 7/7 Bombings

The victims were everyday people – commuters, students, tourists, and workers – just going about their lives. In a matter of moments, their lives were tragically cut short, and the lives of their loved ones were changed forever. These victims did not fit a specific mold. They were people from different backgrounds, races, and religions, reflecting the diversity and vibrancy of London itself.

The victims of the bombings represented a cross-section of British society. They included both London residents and people who had traveled into the city for work or study, many of whom had no prior connection to terrorism or political violence. The youngest victim, 18-year-old Hasib Hussain, had just begun his life as an adult, while the oldest, 60-year-old Mena Trott, had raised children and grandchildren.

THE VICTIMS ON THE UNDERGROUND TRAINS

The first explosion occurred at 8:50 AM on the Circle Line between Aldgate and Liverpool Street stations. This bomb, detonated by Shehzad Tanweer, killed six people. The passengers, who were traveling to work or meeting family and friends, were instantly killed or gravely injured. The chaos that followed was immediate, with injured survivors scrambling to escape from the wreckage of the train.

The second bomb went off at 8:51 AM on the Piccadilly Line between King's Cross and Russell Square stations. This was the most deadly explosion of the three on the Underground, killing 26 people. The bomb exploded in a packed train, and the station, located near King's Cross, became a symbol of the destruction caused by the attack. Among those killed were both Londoners and tourists, including passengers on their way to explore the city's landmarks.

At 8:56 AM, the third explosion occurred on the Hammersmith & City Line between Edgware Road and Paddington stations. This bomb, carried out by Germaine Lindsay, killed seven people. Much like the other explosions, the blast tore through the train, causing widespread injury and panic. The lives of the victims were torn apart in an instant, and the passengers on this train, some of whom had just met up with friends for a day out, found themselves caught in an unimaginable situation.

THE VICTIMS ON THE NUMBER 30 BUS

The final explosion of the 7/7 bombings occurred at 9:47 AM on the number 30 bus in Tavistock Square, near University College Hospital. Hasib Hussain, the youngest of the bombers, detonated his bomb on the bus, killing 13 people. The bus explosion caused immense damage, and the blast was so powerful that the roof of the bus was blown off. The violence of the attack killed victims instantly and left survivors in deep shock. Many of the victims on the bus were elderly, including 60-year-old Mena Trott, who was on her way to a hospital appointment when the bomb went off.

One of the most heart-wrenching aspects of the bus explosion was the sheer randomness of the victims' journeys. Some were on their way to medical appointments, others were on their way to work, while others were simply taking the bus to meet family or friends. There were no distinguishing characteristics among them; they were ordinary people who were united only by the unfortunate circumstance of being in the wrong place at the wrong time.

The blast left a permanent mark on those who survived. Many of the victims had to endure severe physical injuries, such as broken bones, burns, and traumatic head injuries. For some, the emotional scars of the experience are just as painful.

THE SURVIVORS: THE UNSEEN VICTIMS

While much focus is placed on those who tragically lost their lives in the 7/7 bombings, there were many who survived but were left with lifelong physical and psychological scars. These survivors carry the trauma of the bombings with them every day, even years after the attacks.

Some survivors suffered from life-changing injuries that resulted in permanent disabilities. Others bore the emotional scars of losing loved ones in the blink of an eye. Many experienced what is known as post-traumatic stress disorder (PTSD), a mental health condition that can develop after experiencing or witnessing a traumatic event. Survivors have described their experiences as feeling like they were "living in a nightmare," with memories of the blast, the aftermath, and the chaos haunting them long after they had escaped the wreckage.

The survivors also carried the weight of guilt. In the aftermath of the bombings, some survivors felt survivor's guilt, questioning why they had lived while others had died. They often struggled to understand the randomness of the attack and why they had been spared. For many survivors, the bombings reshaped their view of the world and their sense of safety.

THE IMPACT ON FAMILIES AND COMMUNITIES

The families of the victims were left in the depths of grief and mourning. They had lost fathers, mothers, sons, daughters, brothers, and sisters, all in a senseless act of violence. For many families, the loss was not just of a loved one, but the loss of the future they had envisioned for that person. Children who had lost their parents were left to grow up without them, and parents who had lost their children were forced to deal with the immeasurable pain of burying their own offspring.

These families were forced to navigate a range of emotions in the aftermath of the bombings, from anger and disbelief to sorrow and, in some cases, a call for justice. The families of the victims, as well as the survivors, found themselves thrust into the public eye, often dealing with the overwhelming media coverage and public scrutiny. Many families chose to speak out to honor their loved ones and raise awareness of the human cost of terrorism.

Communities that were touched by the attack, particularly those in the areas surrounding the bombing sites, were also deeply affected. Local businesses, schools, and residents experienced the trauma of living in a place where so much devastation had occurred. People felt the loss of their neighbors and friends, and in many ways, the bombings fractured the community spirit that had defined London for so long.

The ripple effects of the bombings also spread beyond London. Victims came from all over the UK, as well as overseas. The global nature of the victims highlighted just how far-reaching the effects of terrorism could be. Families across the world mourned the loss of loved ones and grappled with the realization that terrorism could strike anywhere, even in a city as cosmopolitan and seemingly safe as London.

REMEMBERING THE VICTIMS

In the aftermath of the attacks, memorial services and commemorations were held for the victims. Public memorials, such as the unveiling of a plaque in Hyde Park and tributes at King's Cross Station, became places where survivors and family members could pay their respects to those who had died. The victims' names were read aloud, and their memories were honored in moments of silence.

The legacy of the victims of 7/7 extends beyond memorials. Their lives and their stories continue to shape the national conversation around terrorism and counterterrorism. Their deaths prompted widespread calls for greater cooperation in fighting extremism, greater attention to mental health issues, and a renewed focus on community cohesion. The victims are remembered not only as symbols of the tragedy but also as human beings who led ordinary lives that were abruptly and unfairly cut short.

THE AFTERMATH: SHOCK AND GRIEF

In the immediate aftermath of the bombings, London and the United Kingdom were in shock. The scale of the attack was unlike anything seen in the country before. The loss of life and the extent of the injuries left a profound impact on the city and the nation as a whole. People of all backgrounds came together to offer support to the victims, and memorial services were held across London.

However, the attacks also sparked a wave of anxiety and fear across the UK, particularly within Muslim communities. Many Muslims in Britain faced increased scrutiny and suspicion, and there was a rise in Islamophobic attacks following 7/7. The bombings served to deepen the divisions between different groups within British society, leading to debates about integration, radicalization, and the role of foreign policy in fostering terrorism.

In the days and weeks following the attack, Londoners returned to work, used public transportation again, and showed resilience. But the shadow of the bombings loomed large. The city's transport system, the symbol of London's openness and accessibility, had been violated in a way that was hard to comprehend.

THE INVESTIGATION: UNCOVERING THE TRUTH

The investigation into the bombings was a monumental task for the British police. The authorities had to identify the perpetrators, understand the logistics of the attack, and determine the broader network behind the bombings. Forensic evidence, CCTV footage, and witness testimony were crucial in piecing together the events of that fateful morning.

Within days, investigators had identified the four bombers through CCTV footage. The surveillance cameras in the London Underground and on buses provided vital clues. The men's movements were tracked from the time they entered the stations to the moment they detonated their explosives. The fact that these men were British citizens shocked many, as it indicated that terrorism could emerge from within the very fabric of British society.

The investigation also revealed that the bombers had been influenced by extremist ideology, and it was believed they had been inspired by al-Qaeda's teachings. Although the bombers acted alone, they were part of a wider network of radical individuals who had been involved in organizing training, acquiring explosives, and spreading extremist views.

In the aftermath of the bombings, the UK government and law enforcement agencies implemented a range of new counterterrorism measures. These included increased surveillance, tighter security on public transport, and more stringent regulations on extremist content online. While these measures were designed to prevent future attacks, they also sparked debates about civil liberties and the balance between security and freedom.

THE LEGACY: A CHANGED SOCIETY

The 7/7 bombings left an indelible mark on London and the United Kingdom. They exposed vulnerabilities in the country's security infrastructure and prompted widespread discussions about national identity, immigration, and integration. The bombings also led to a reevaluation of Britain's foreign policy, particularly its involvement in Iraq and Afghanistan, which had been cited as a motivating factor for the attackers.

In the years following 7/7, Britain's counterterrorism policies became more stringent. The government introduced the Terrorism Act 2006, which gave police expanded powers to deal with suspected terrorists. In addition, the UK focused more on preventing radicalization through community outreach programs, especially in areas with large Muslim populations.

The legacy of 7/7 also includes ongoing efforts to promote interfaith dialogue, foster community cohesion, and prevent the spread of extremist ideologies. Survivors of the bombings have worked tirelessly to promote peace and understanding in the wake of the attack, while families of the victims continue to honor their loved ones' memory through charitable endeavors and public service.

CONCLUSION

The 7/7 bombings were a dark and defining moment in British history. The coordinated attacks shattered the sense of security that had long been associated with London and revealed the dangers of radicalization within society. The bombers, driven by their extremist beliefs, sought to make a statement, but their actions left a lasting impact on the lives of the victims, their families, and the wider public.

The aftermath of the bombings changed the way Britain approached issues of terrorism, counterterrorism, and national security. In the years that followed, the country implemented a range of measures to prevent future attacks and to address the root causes of radicalization. The events of 7/7 continue to resonate in the UK and around the world, serving as a reminder of the need to confront extremism and to work towards a more inclusive, tolerant society.

CHAPTER 4
9/11 TWIN TOWER ATTACKS
AN ACT OF PURE EVIL

Smoke Pours From The Twin Towers

The events of September 11, 2001, when the World Trade Center towers in New York City were destroyed by terrorist attacks, remain a defining moment in modern history. The attack, known as the 9/11 attacks, led to the deaths of nearly 3,000 people and changed the world in profound ways. It set the stage for global conflicts, the War on Terror, the creation of the Department of Homeland Security, and major shifts in foreign and domestic policies. This account will delve into the roots of the 9/11 attacks, the events leading up to the day itself, and the aftermath of the attacks, with a focus on the key players, motivations, and actions that culminated in that fateful day.

ROOTS OF THE 9/11 ATTACKS-RISE OF AL-QAEDA

The roots of the 9/11 attacks lie in the complex geopolitics of the Middle East in the late 20th century. One of the most important factors in the rise of Al-Qaeda was the 1979 Soviet invasion of Afghanistan. In response to the invasion, the United States, along with its allies, supported Afghan resistance fighters (known as the Mujahideen) with funding, arms, and training. This was part of the broader Cold War strategy of containing Soviet expansionism. Among those who rose to prominence during this conflict was Osama bin Laden, a wealthy Saudi national who had come to Afghanistan to fight against the Soviets and support the Afghan cause.

Bin Laden's time in Afghanistan and his experiences with other Islamic fighters led him to adopt a radical interpretation of Islam. He viewed the United States and its allies as the primary enemies of Islam, due to their military presence in the Middle East and their support for authoritarian regimes in the region, particularly in countries like Saudi Arabia and Egypt. In 1988, bin Laden formed Al-Qaeda (meaning "the base") as a network to continue his jihad, or holy war, against the West and corrupt Muslim governments that he saw as illegitimate.

Al-Qaeda's ideology was rooted in a belief that the West, led by the U.S., was attempting to destroy Islam and that violent jihad was necessary to defend Muslim lands. Bin Laden and his followers saw themselves as engaged in a global struggle against "infidels" and "apostates," a view that would later motivate their decision to attack the United States directly.

U.S. FOREIGN POLICY AND BIN LADEN'S GROWING HATRED

Osama bin Laden's anger at the United States was exacerbated by several key events in the 1990s. One of the most significant of these was the Gulf War in 1990-1991. After Iraq's invasion of Kuwait, the United States led a military coalition to expel Saddam Hussein's forces. A major component of the U.S. strategy was the deployment of U.S. military personnel to Saudi Arabia, the birthplace of Islam, which Bin Laden viewed as a desecration of sacred land. In his mind, the presence of U.S. troops in the kingdom was an affront to Islam.

In the years following the Gulf War, Al-Qaeda's rhetoric became increasingly anti-Western and anti-American. Bin Laden's declaration of war against the United States in 1996 outlined his grievances, accusing the U.S. of being the primary enemy of Islam due to its foreign policy in the Middle East, including its support for Israel, its military presence in Saudi Arabia, and its sanctions against Iraq. In 1998, Al-Qaeda's leadership issued a fatwa, or religious edict, calling for Muslims to kill Americans and their allies in an effort to expel them from Muslim lands.

The increasing animosity between the United States and Al-Qaeda escalated as the latter grew more audacious in its actions. Al-Qaeda carried out attacks against U.S. interests in the late 1990s, including the bombings of U.S. embassies in Kenya and Tanzania in 1998, which killed over 200 people. The 2000 bombing of the USS Cole, a U.S. Navy destroyer, in Yemen, which killed 17 American sailors, further heightened tensions.

THE PATH TO 9/11

By the late 1990s, Osama bin Laden's global jihadist network had grown increasingly sophisticated. Al-Qaeda had become a transnational organization with cells operating in numerous countries. One of the key figures in Al-Qaeda's planning for 9/11 was Khalid Sheikh Mohammed (KSM), a Pakistani national who had been involved in several previous terrorist plots against the U.S., including the 1993 bombing of the World Trade Center. Mohammed had spent years cultivating the idea of using a hijacking as a method for carrying out a devastating attack on U.S. soil. In the mid-1990s, KSM presented his plan to Osama bin Laden: hijack commercial airplanes and crash them into symbolic U.S. targets, causing maximum destruction.

Initially, bin Laden was reluctant to approve the plan, but over time, he became convinced of its potential. The 9/11 plot was born in the context of the growing radicalization within Al-Qaeda, which saw the destruction of the World Trade Center and the Pentagon as the ultimate statement of defiance against the West. KSM was appointed as the mastermind of the operation, and in the years that followed, he began recruiting individuals and organizing the logistics for what would become the deadliest terrorist attack in history.

RECRUITMENT OF HIJACKERS

The planning for 9/11 began in earnest in 1999 when Khalid Sheikh Mohammed began recruiting individuals who would carry out the hijackings. Most of the hijackers were young men from Saudi Arabia, Egypt, and other countries in the Middle East, many of whom had lived in Western countries and were familiar with the culture and practices of the U.S. The group's leader, Mohamed Atta, was an Egyptian national with a background in civil engineering who had come to the United States for pilot training. He was selected to lead the hijackers because of his ability to blend in, his air-pilot skills, and his commitment to the Al-Qaeda ideology.

The hijackers were divided into four groups, each of which would take control of one of the four airplanes. Atta, along with other hijackers like Marwan al-Shehhi, Ziad Jarrah, and Hani Hanjour, would pilot the planes. In total, 19 men were selected to carry out the attacks, and they received training on how to hijack commercial airliners and overcome their flight crews.

The planning involved extensive coordination between Al-Qaeda operatives in various countries. Training took place in Afghanistan and other parts of the world, and a network of facilitators helped ensure that the hijackers obtained the necessary resources, including plane tickets, fake identification, and weapons.

THE ROLE OF AFGHANISTAN AND THE TALIBAN

The Taliban, which had come to power in Afghanistan in the mid-1990s, played a significant role in the events leading up to 9/11. The group was a close ally of Osama bin Laden, who had been given refuge in Afghanistan after being expelled from Sudan. While the Taliban's role in the 9/11 attacks was indirect, their support for bin Laden provided the safe haven and infrastructure that allowed Al-Qaeda to operate with relative impunity.

The U.S. had pressured the Taliban to expel bin Laden, but the regime refused, citing their ideological alliance with him. The inability to stop Al-Qaeda's activities in Afghanistan meant that bin Laden and his network had a free hand to carry out attacks and train operatives, culminating in the 9/11 attacks.

U.S. INTELLIGENCE AND MISSED WARNINGS

In the years leading up to the 9/11 attacks, the U.S. intelligence community became increasingly aware of the growing threat posed by Al-Qaeda. There were numerous warnings about the possibility of an attack, but these warnings were fragmented and did not lead to decisive action. In particular, intelligence agencies were unable to piece together the details of the plot before it was too late.

One of the most significant missed opportunities was the failure to track the movement of the hijackers, many of whom had been in the U.S. for months prior to the attack. The FBI and CIA had some information about these individuals, but coordination between the agencies was lacking. The so-called "wall" between intelligence agencies, which made it difficult for them to share information, was one of the key factors that hindered the U.S. response.

In the months leading up to the attacks, there were several incidents that should have raised alarm bells. In August 2001, the CIA intercepted a message indicating that Al-Qaeda was planning something big, but the specifics were unclear. This warning, along with other intelligence, was not acted upon with the urgency that was required.

THE DAY OF THE 9/11 ATTACKS

The morning of September 11, 2001, began as any other Tuesday in the United States. However, by the end of the day, the world would be forever changed. The coordinated terrorist attacks orchestrated by Al-Qaeda resulted in the deaths of nearly 3,000 people and sent shockwaves around the globe, leading to a global war on terrorism and reshaping U.S. foreign and domestic policy. The story of that day is one of terror, heroism, and tragedy.

EARLY MORNING: THE CALM BEFORE THE STORM

On the morning of September 11, 2001, most Americans began their day like any other. The weather in New York City, Washington, D.C., and other parts of the Northeast was clear and sunny. People were heading to work, children were preparing for school, and no one had any inkling of the tragedy that was about to unfold.

Across the United States, airports were bustling with travelers, with four flights — American Airlines Flight 11, United Airlines Flight 175, American Airlines Flight 77, and United Airlines Flight 93 — all scheduled to take off in the early morning hours.

At 8:00 AM, American Airlines Flight 11 took off from Logan International Airport in Boston, Massachusetts, bound for Los Angeles, California. United Airlines Flight 175 followed shortly, departing from the same airport just 15 minutes later. On the other side of the country, at Washington Dulles International Airport, American Airlines Flight 77 took off at 8:20 AM, also heading to Los Angeles. United Airlines Flight 93, scheduled to depart from Newark International Airport at 8:00 AM, was slightly delayed, taking off at 8:42 AM. These four flights would become the instruments of a horrific terrorist plot that would claim thousands of lives.

THE HIJACKINGS: A COORDINATED ATTACK

By 8:14 AM, American Airlines Flight 11, a Boeing 767 with 92 people aboard, was hijacked. The hijackers took control of the cockpit, killing the flight crew, and began their mission to carry out their planned attack. The passengers and crew on board were unaware of the hijacking for several minutes, but once they realized what was happening, some passengers began making phone calls to loved ones and authorities, providing key information to law enforcement.

At 8:19 AM, Flight 11's flight attendant, Betty Ong, made a call to American Airlines headquarters, describing the hijacking and alerting authorities that the plane had been taken over. She reported that the passengers were in the back of the plane and that there was a serious situation on board. Her final words were chilling: "We are flying very low, we are flying very low."

Just five minutes later, at 8:24 AM, the hijackers turned off the plane's transponder, making it harder for authorities to track its location. The plane, which had been flying at cruising altitude, was now descending rapidly. In the following moments, the hijackers began their deadly mission, preparing to crash the plane into one of the most iconic symbols of American capitalism — the World Trade Center.

At 8:42 AM, United Airlines Flight 175, also a Boeing 767, took off from Boston. This plane, with 65 people on board, was also hijacked by a team of Al-Qaeda operatives. Unlike the first hijacking, passengers on Flight 175 became aware of the hijacking almost immediately. One of the flight attendants, Amy Sweeney, had tried to relay information about the hijacking to the ground crew but was unable to give a precise location of the plane. As

Flight 175 continued its flight, the hijackers took control of the cockpit and began heading toward the World Trade Center.

At 8:51 AM, American Airlines Flight 77, a Boeing 757, took off from Washington Dulles International Airport, bound for Los Angeles. This flight, with 64 people on board, was hijacked 31 minutes later, as the plane was flying over Ohio. The hijackers took control of the cockpit, and the plane made a sharp turn back toward Washington, D.C. At this point, the hijackers' target was clear — the Pentagon.

At 8:42 AM, United Airlines Flight 93, a Boeing 757, had taken off from Newark International Airport. The flight, scheduled to travel from Newark to San Francisco, was also hijacked by four Al-Qaeda operatives. However, unlike the other three flights, the passengers on Flight 93 fought back, heroically attempting to retake control of the plane. While the hijackers' plan was to target a government building in Washington, D.C., the passengers' efforts led to a struggle in the cockpit, causing the plane to crash into a field in Shanksville, Pennsylvania, at 10:03 AM.

THE IMPACT: THE WORLD TRADE CENTER ATTACKS

At 8:46 AM, American Airlines Flight 11 crashed into the North Tower of the World Trade Center in New York City. The impact was catastrophic, as the Boeing 767, traveling at over 400 miles per hour, struck the building between the 93rd and 99th floors, instantly killing hundreds of people. The explosion and subsequent fireball were visible from miles away. The crash sent shockwaves through the city, and emergency responders were immediately dispatched to the scene. Within minutes, both the New York Police Department and Fire Department began arriving at the scene, preparing for what would soon become one of the most deadly and devastating terrorist attacks in U.S. history.

At 9:03 AM, 17 minutes after the North Tower was struck, United Airlines Flight 175 crashed into the South Tower of the World Trade Center. The impact, similar to the first attack, sent another massive explosion through the building. The scene was chaotic. People on the streets below watched in horror as the two buildings — symbols of global finance — burned. Smoke poured from the towers, and debris fell to the ground, killing pedestrians and people in nearby buildings.

By this time, the reality of the situation was becoming apparent to many. It was not just a tragic accident — the World Trade Center was under deliberate attack. News broadcasts across the world showed the images of the burning towers, and the nation's leadership scrambled to respond.

THE PENTAGON ATTACK

While the world's attention was focused on the World Trade Center, another plane was on its deadly mission. American Airlines Flight 77, after being hijacked and redirected toward Washington, D.C., crashed into the Pentagon at 9:37 AM. The Pentagon, the headquarters of the United States Department of Defense, is one of the most protected buildings in the world. However, the hijackers' plane, which struck the western side of the building, caused a tremendous explosion that killed 125 people inside the Pentagon, along with all 64 people on board the flight.

The impact of Flight 77 caused a massive fire that quickly spread through the building, and parts of the outer structure collapsed. Emergency responders rushed to the scene to save those trapped in the rubble. In Washington, D.C., the enormity of the attacks was becoming clear, and airspace was quickly closed, with military jets being scrambled to protect the capital.

THE HEROIC EFFORT ON FLIGHT 93

At 10:03 AM, the hijacked United Airlines Flight 93 crashed into a field near Shanksville, Pennsylvania, after passengers and crew members fought the hijackers. The flight, which had been en route to San Francisco, was headed toward Washington, D.C., with the likely target being the White House or the U.S. Capitol. The passengers on board had learned of the previous attacks via phone calls and were determined not to let their plane become another weapon.

In a desperate attempt to regain control of the plane, the passengers stormed the cockpit, engaging in a violent struggle with the hijackers. The plane ultimately crashed into a field, killing all 40 people on board. Their heroism prevented an even greater catastrophe, saving countless lives in Washington, D.C., although they paid the ultimate price in doing so.

THE COLLAPSE OF THE TOWERS

As the morning wore on, the destruction caused by the attacks continued to unfold. The fires caused by the impact of the planes had weakened the structural integrity of the World Trade Center towers. At 9:59 AM, the South Tower, which had been struck by Flight 175, collapsed after burning for 56 minutes. The collapse was devastating, sending tons of debris crashing into the streets below, obliterating everything in its path.

At 10:28 AM, the North Tower, which had been burning for over an hour, also collapsed. The collapse of the second tower was a moment of sheer horror for those who had been watching the tragedy unfold. The loss of the two iconic towers, once the tallest buildings in New York, marked the physical and symbolic destruction of a central part of American identity.

The collapse of the World Trade Center towers was followed by a massive rescue and recovery operation, as first responders, including firefighters, police officers, and paramedics, worked in the rubble in a desperate attempt to find survivors. However, the scale of the destruction was so severe that the search quickly turned into a recovery effort.

THE IMMEDIATE AFTERMATH AND NATIONAL RESPONSE

By the time the dust had settled, the full scale of the attacks had become clear. Nearly 3,000 people were dead, including passengers on the four hijacked planes, workers in the Twin Towers, emergency responders, and military personnel at the Pentagon. The attacks left a deep scar on the American psyche.

President George W. Bush, who was in Sarasota, Florida, at the time of the attacks, was informed of the situation while visiting a classroom. He remained calm, listening to details about the unfolding crisis. At 9:30 AM, he made his first public statement, calling the attacks "evil" and promising to bring those responsible to justice.

At 10:30 AM, the White House and Capitol Hill were evacuated as authorities feared more planes were headed toward Washington. Later that day, President Bush addressed the nation, vowing that the United States would strike back against those responsible for the attacks.

CONCLUSION: THE DAY THAT CHANGED THE WORLD

The events of September 11, 2001, were a devastating act of terrorism that shattered the sense of security that many Americans had taken for granted. The coordinated hijackings, the attacks on the World Trade Center and the Pentagon, and the heroism shown by the passengers on Flight 93 are forever etched in the memory of the world. The attacks on 9/11 were not only an assault on American soil but also an assault on the very values of freedom and democracy that the United States represents.

In the aftermath of the attacks, the United States embarked on a new era of security measures, international military interventions, and a long-standing conflict known as the War on Terror. The memory of 9/11 remains a central event in modern history, shaping U.S. foreign policy and the global response to terrorism for decades to come.

CHAPTER 5
GAMBINO CRIME CARTEL
RISE AND FALL OF THE NEW YORK DRUG KINGS

John Gotti

The Gambino family, once one of the most notorious and powerful Mafia families in America an history, has been at the center of organized crime in New York City for decades. From its origins in the early 1900s to its peak under the leadership of John Gotti, the family's crimes spanned a wide array of illicit activities, including murder, extortion, drug trafficking, racketeering, and more. We explore the history of the Gambino family, its rise to power, the notorious crimes committed by its members, and the ultimate downfall of its leaders.

THE ORIGINS OF THE GAMBINO FAMILY

The story of the Gambino family begins in the early 1900s, but the family's real influence in the world of organized crime did not begin until the 1950s. The family traces its roots to a Sicilian immigrant named Salvatore "Toto" D'Aquila, who was born in Sicily and immigrated to New York in the early 1900s. D'Aquila was one of the first key figures in the formation of the family, involved in illegal activities like bootlegging, extortion, and gambling. He played a significant role in the early years of organized crime in New York, and his influence would pave the way for the Gambino family's later power.

NEW YORK GANGS[

By 1910, more Italian gangs had formed in New York City. In addition to the original Morello gang in East Harlem and D'Aquila's own, now growing gang, also in East Harlem (but expanding into Little Italy in Manhattan's Lower East Side), there were other organizations forming. In Brooklyn, Nicole "Cola" Schiro established a second gang of Sicilian mafiosi from Castekkanmare de Golfo, west of Palermo, in Sicily. A third Sicilian gang was formed by Alfred Minor in Brooklyn. Another Morello captain, Gaetano Reina, had also broken away in the Bronx, ruling that area with impunity. In south Brooklyn, first Johhny Torrio, then Frankie Yale, were leading a new and rising organization. Finally, there were two allied Neapolitan Camorra gangs, one on Coney Island, and one on Navy Street in Brooklyn, that were run by Pellegrino Morano and Alessandro Vollero.

In 1916 the Camorra had assassinated Nicholas Morello, head of the Morello gang. In response, D'Aquila allied with the Morellos to fight the Camorra. In 1917, both Morano and Vollero were convicted of murder and sentenced to life in prison. With their leadership gone, the two Camorra gangs disappeared and D'Aquila and the Schiro family in Brooklyn took over many of their rackets in Brooklyn. Soon after, D'Aquila absorbed the Mineo gang, making Mineo his first lieutenant. D'Aquila now controlled the largest and most influential Italian gang in New York City. It was about this time that Masseria, another former Morello captain, began asserting his influence over the Lower East Side's Little Italy and began to come into conflict with D'Aquila's operations there, as Prohibition approached.

PROHIBITION

In 1920, the United States outlawed the production and sale of alcoholic beverages, creating the opportunity for an extremely lucrative illegal racket for the New York gangs.

By 1920, D'Aquila's only significant rival was Guiseppe "Joe the Boss" Masseria. Masseria had taken over the Morello family interests, and by the mid-1920s, had begun to amass power and influence to rival that of D'Aquila. By the late 1920s, D'Aquila and Masseria were headed for a showdown.

On October 10, 1928, Masseria gunmen assassinated Salvatore D'Aquila outside his home. D'Aquila's second-in-command, Alfred Mineo and his right-hand man, Steve Ferrigino now commanded the largest and most influential Sicilian gang in New York City.

However, the real rise of the family began after the death of D'Aquila in 1928. This opened the door for a power struggle among various Mafia families, with the most influential Mafia families in New York vying for control over lucrative criminal enterprises. In the early years, the family was initially known as the "Gambino" family after one of its early bosses, Carlo Gambino.

CARLO GAMBINO – THE ARCHITECT OF THE FAMILY'S POWER

Carlo Gambino became the official boss of the family in the early 1950s after a series of violent events and strategic maneuverings. Gambino had come from humble beginnings in Sicily, and his rise to power was methodical. Unlike other Mafia bosses of the time, Carlo Gambino was known for his ability to avoid attention, work quietly behind the scenes, and ensure the family's power while keeping a low profile.

Carlo Gambino's reign marked a turning point for the family. Under his leadership, the family's criminal activities expanded significantly. Gambino focused on traditional Mafia rackets such as extortion, loansharking, and control of labor unions. However, his greatest legacy was the way he handled relationships with other organized crime families. Gambino established powerful alliances with other Mafia bosses, avoiding conflict and ensuring a constant flow of income for the family.

Carlo's shrewdness allowed the Gambino family to prosper, but it also set the stage for future violence and criminal acts that would define the family's criminal legacy.

THE GAMBINO FAMILY UNDER JOHN GOTTI

While Carlo Gambino was a mastermind of Mafia operations, it was his successor, John Gotti, who turned the Gambino family into a household name. Gotti was a notorious figure, whose criminal activities and lavish lifestyle made him one of the most well-known mobsters in American history.

JOHN GOTTI'S RISE TO POWER

John Gotti was born in 1940 in the neighborhood of Ozone Park, Queens, New York. He grew up in an environment steeped in poverty, which ultimately led him to a life of crime. Gotti's first major crime was his involvement in petty theft and small-time street-level hustles. However, he quickly rose through the ranks of the Gambino family, gaining recognition for his ruthlessness and his ability to handle business dealings in a brutal manner.

Gotti's path to becoming boss of the Gambino family was marked by violence and strategic maneuvering. In 1976, Gotti played a key role in the assassination of a high-ranking Gambino family member, James McBratney. McBratney had murdered the family's previous boss, and Gotti's involvement in McBratney's death earned him a reputation as a skilled and loyal hitman. He became known for his work as an enforcer, carrying out orders with precision and fearlessness.

However, Gotti's most well-known act was his role in the assassination of Paul Castellano, the boss of the Gambino family at the time. Castellano had taken over the family after Carlo Gambino's death in 1976, but his leadership was seen as weak and disconnected from the traditional Mafia operations. Gotti believed that Castellano's management of the family was detrimental to its interests, and he made the bold decision to have Castellano killed.

On December 16, 1985, Paul Castellano and his underboss, Thomas Bilotti, were shot and killed outside the Sparks Steakhouse in Manhattan. The hit was meticulously planned by Gotti and his associates. By killing Castellano, Gotti not only took control of the Gambino family, but he also solidified his place as the new boss of one of New York's most powerful criminal organizations.

GOTTI'S REIGN: THE RISE OF A MOB ICON

With Gotti at the helm, the Gambino family became an unstoppable force in organized crime. Gotti's violent and aggressive tactics ensured that the family expanded its operations into various criminal enterprises. Under his leadership, the family ran a massive network of rackets, including drug trafficking, gambling, extortion, loan sharking, and labor union corruption. The Gambino family's reach extended into legitimate businesses as well, such as construction companies, where they extorted workers and used their influence to manipulate contracts.

Gotti's lifestyle was also infamous. He was known for his flashy clothes, expensive cars, and his public persona as the "Dapper Don." His ability to avoid conviction despite numerous criminal charges earned him the nickname "The Teflon Don." Gotti's skill in evading conviction was largely due to his ability to intimidate witnesses and manipulate the legal system. In the mid-1980s, Gotti was arrested for the murder of Castellano, but he was acquitted in 1987, in part due to his ability to intimidate witnesses and orchestrate a high-profile trial.

However, Gotti's reign would eventually come to an end, due in large part to his overconfidence and reckless behavior. Despite his success in avoiding the law, Gotti made enemies within the Mafia and beyond. His most significant enemy was Salvatore "Sammy the Bull" Gravano, the Gambino family's underboss, who became disgruntled with Gotti's leadership.

THE CRIMES OF THE GAMBINO FAMILY

The Gambino family was involved in a staggering array of criminal activities during its reign. These activities were not limited to street-level hustles but extended into large-scale, organized operations that spanned both illegal and legitimate enterprises.

Murder and Violence

At the heart of the Gambino family's operations was murder. Whether it was the assassination of rival mobsters, enemies, or those who had betrayed the family, murder was an essential tool in maintaining power. The family's murders were often carried out in cold blood and with the approval of the higher-ups.

The murder of Paul Castellano was the most high-profile example of the family's violence, but it was by no means the only one. Numerous other murders, including the killing of informants and traitors within the family, marked the Gambino family's bloody history.

Drug Trafficking and Racketeering

Under Gotti's leadership, the Gambino family expanded its operations into drug trafficking, a sector that had been traditionally avoided by Mafia families due to the risk of attracting federal attention. However, the family's need for increased revenue led them to begin smuggling heroin, cocaine, and other drugs into the United States. The family worked with international drug cartels, and their distribution networks extended across the country.

The Gambinos also engaged in traditional Mafia rackets, such as extortion, loan sharking, and the manipulation of labor unions. They controlled a wide array of businesses, often forcing small business owners to pay for "protection" or be subjected to violence. Their influence over unions allowed them to steal money from workers and manipulate building contracts to benefit the family.

Money Laundering and Legitimate Businesses

Like other Mafia families, the Gambinos used legitimate businesses as fronts for their criminal operations. They owned and operated construction companies, nightclubs, restaurants, and other businesses, all of which were used to launder money obtained through illegal activities. Through these businesses, the family could move money, avoid detection, and gain access to powerful people in both business and politics.

THE FALL OF JOHN GOTTI

Despite his seemingly invincible status, Gotti's downfall came from within his own ranks. Sammy Gravano, the underboss, became disillusioned with Gotti's leadership and his increasing arrogance. Gravano, seeking to secure his own future, agreed to cooperate with the FBI and testify against Gotti.

In 1992, Gotti was convicted of murder, racketeering, and other crimes. His conviction was based on the testimony of Gravano, who became one of the most infamous mob turncoats in history. With Gotti's conviction, the Gambino family lost its most influential leader.

Gotti was sentenced to life in prison, where he would eventually die in 2002. His downfall was a significant blow to the Gambino family, and while the family still exists today, its power has been greatly diminished.

THE LEGACY OF THE GAMBINO FAMILY

The Gambino family's history is a story of violence, greed, and betrayal. From its early days under Carlo Gambino to its peak under John Gotti, the family amassed significant wealth and power through a range of criminal activities. However, their ultimate downfall shows the dangers of organized crime – even the most powerful families can be brought down by betrayal from within.

Despite the arrests, convictions, and ongoing investigations, the Gambino family continues to exist today, albeit in a diminished state. It remains a symbol of organized crime in America, its legacy ingrained in the history of the Mafia.

As the world continues to evolve, the Gambino family's past serves as a cautionary tale of the consequences of a life of crime, and the families, victims, and communities affected by their actions.

CHAPTER 6
MANCHESTER ARENA BOMBING
THE SENSELESS KILLING OF INNOCENTS

Manchester Arena

The Manchester Arena bombing refers to the tragic terrorist attack that took place on the evening of May 22, 2017, at the Manchester Arena in Manchester, England. The bombing occurred during a concert by American pop singer Ariana Grande, as thousands of fans were leaving the venue. It was a horrific event that claimed 22 innocent lives, injured hundreds more, and left a lasting impact on the city and the wider world. This attack, which was later attributed to Islamist extremist Salman Abedi, shook the United Kingdom and led to significant discussions around security, counterterrorism measures, and the wider implications of terrorism on society. The following is an in-depth exploration of the attack, the perpetrator, the aftermath, and its broader implications.

BACKGROUND: MANCHESTER ARENA

The Manchester Arena is one of the largest indoor arenas in the United Kingdom. Located in the heart of the city, it is a multi-purpose venue, known for hosting concerts, sporting events, and various live performances. At the time of the bombing, the arena had been hosting an Ariana Grande concert as part of her Dangerous Woman Tour. The event was packed with people, many of whom were young fans attending with family and friends. As the concert ended, the venue quickly became a scene of chaos, confusion, and devastation.

The arena, with a capacity of 21,000, was one of the busiest and most well-known concert venues in the UK. Because of its size and popularity, it was a high-profile target for terrorist groups seeking to inflict maximum casualties and generate widespread media attention. The venue was designed with modern security measures, but like many large venues, it was still vulnerable to coordinated attacks.

THE PERPETRATOR: SALMAN ABEDI

The perpetrator of the Manchester Arena bombing was Salman Abedi, a 22-year-old British man of Libyan descent. Abedi was born on December 31, 1994, in Manchester, to parents who had emigrated from Libya in the 1990s. His family lived in the southern part of the city, and he was reportedly well known in the local community. However, Abedi's life took a troubling turn in his late teens. He became involved with extremist ideology, and in the years leading up to the bombing, he showed increasing signs of radicalization.

Abedi's background was complex. He had attended the University of Salford but dropped out before completing his studies. He had also spent time in Libya, which is believed to have influenced his extremist views. It was during these trips abroad, including one just weeks before the attack, that he is thought to have become more radicalized. Abedi's radicalization process was reportedly facilitated by his exposure to jihadist propaganda and his association with known extremists in Manchester. He is believed to have been in contact with individuals linked to terrorist organizations, including ISIS (the Islamic State of Iraq and Syria), who had influenced his actions leading up to the attack.

Before the bombing, Abedi had been in the process of assembling the bomb used in the attack. It was later discovered that he had constructed an improvised explosive device (IED) with a large quantity of nails and other shrapnel to maximize the destructive power of the blast. On the night of the attack, Abedi took his bomb to the Arena, where he detonated it in the foyer area, close to the exit doors. This area was particularly crowded with concertgoers, making it the ideal location for him to cause the maximum amount of devastation.

THE ATTACK

On May 22, 2017, at approximately 10:31 p.m., as the Ariana Grande concert came to a close, Salman Abedi detonated his bomb. The blast occurred just outside the arena's main auditorium in the North Foyer area, a section of the venue that was especially crowded with concertgoers exiting the building. The explosion killed 22 people, ranging in age from 8 to 51 years old, and injured more than 100 others, with many sustaining life-changing injuries. The explosion was a horrific and brutal act of terrorism.

The blast caused widespread panic and confusion. People who had been inside the concert hall were thrown into chaos as they attempted to flee the venue. Emergency services were quickly mobilized, with police, ambulances, and fire services responding to the scene. However, the explosion created significant obstacles for responders, with debris and crowds making it difficult to access the area quickly. The situation was further complicated by the fact that Abedi had not only killed and injured many people in the explosion but had also targeted the exit area, where people were vulnerable.

In the aftermath of the bombing, it was reported that many concertgoers had helped each other, with bystanders rushing to assist the wounded and offer support to those in shock. The images of young children and families devastated by the attack captured the emotional toll of the event. As the scale of the tragedy became clear, the country was left in mourning.

The attack was claimed by ISIS, who hailed Abedi as a "martyr" for his actions. This claim, though not unusual for terror organizations, served to highlight the growing threat of Islamist extremism within the UK and other Western nations. Authorities soon launched an extensive investigation into Abedi's background, his connections, and his activities leading up to the attack.

THE INVESTIGATION

Following the bombing, law enforcement agencies immediately launched a wide-reaching investigation to identify those responsible for the attack and prevent any further threats. The investigation was one of the largest and most complex in recent UK history. The police sought to determine how Abedi had obtained the materials for the bomb, how he was radicalized, and whether anyone had assisted him in planning the attack.

In the days following the bombing, several people were arrested in connection with the attack. Investigators believed that Abedi had been in contact with individuals who had helped him with logistics, such as purchasing bomb-making materials. However, despite extensive efforts, only a few individuals were charged with terrorism offenses in relation to the bombing. Abedi himself was killed in the explosion, making it impossible for law enforcement to interrogate him or gain further insight into his motivations and contacts.

The investigation also shed light on the deficiencies in the intelligence and counterterrorism systems in place at the time. For instance, it was revealed that Abedi had been flagged by intelligence agencies in the past, but due to a lack of coordination between agencies and resources, he had not been sufficiently monitored. This raised important questions about how authorities could prevent future attacks and respond more effectively to emerging threats.

LEGAL AND POLITICAL IMPLICATIONS

The Manchester Arena bombing raised several legal and political issues that continue to be discussed in the UK today. One of the main issues was the question of preventing radicalization. Despite growing concerns about Islamist extremism, there were still many gaps in the UK's counterterrorism strategy, especially when it came to identifying and monitoring individuals like Salman Abedi. In response to the bombing, there was a renewed focus on intelligence sharing, counter-radicalization programs, and community engagement as key components of national security.

Additionally, the UK government faced pressure to improve public safety and increase security measures at major venues and events. While the Manchester Arena bombing was a tragic reminder of the vulnerability of large public gatherings, it also led to calls for improved venue security, including more rigorous checks on bags and increased awareness of potential terrorist threats. Public and private sectors alike began investing in better security technologies, personnel training, and coordination to prevent future attacks.

THE BROADER IMPACT OF THE MANCHESTER ARENA BOMBING

The Manchester Arena bombing had far-reaching effects, not just on the city and the UK, but on the global fight against terrorism. It highlighted the growing threat posed by homegrown terrorism, with individuals radicalized within their own communities. It also raised questions about the challenges of preventing lone-wolf attacks, in which individuals act alone but are inspired by extremist ideologies.

The bombing also cast a spotlight on the mental health impact of terrorism. Survivors of the attack, as well as the families of the victims, were left with long-term emotional trauma. Many individuals reported suffering from post-traumatic stress disorder (PTSD), anxiety, and depression in the wake of the attack. The attack, therefore, underscored the importance of providing mental health support for those affected by terrorism and conflict.

In the years that followed, the Manchester Arena bombing became a symbol of both the horror of terrorism and the resilience of the human spirit. The One Love Manchester benefit concert, which was held just weeks after the attack and featured performances by artists like Ariana Grande, Coldplay, and Justin Bieber, raised millions for the victims and their families. It also sent a powerful message of solidarity, love, and unity in the face of violence.

THE AFTERMATH AND LONG-TERM EFFECTS OF THE ATTACK

In the wake of the Manchester Arena bombing, the aftermath reverberated across both local and international communities. The emotional and psychological effects of the attack, coupled with the investigative work and political responses, underscored the complexity of such tragic events and their long-term consequences. The bomb left more than physical destruction in its wake — it influenced political decisions, security policies, societal attitudes, and public perceptions of safety in public spaces.

THE EMOTIONAL IMPACT ON VICTIMS AND FAMILIES

The human cost of the attack was staggering. In addition to the 22 lives lost, many survivors of the bombing faced physical and emotional scars that would last a lifetime. Some individuals sustained severe injuries, including amputations, burns, and other debilitating wounds. Others suffered from the psychological toll of the attack, with post-traumatic stress disorder (PTSD), anxiety, depression, and survivor's guilt becoming common issues for those who were directly affected by the bombing.

Victims ranged from young children to elderly adults, with many families enduring the unimaginable pain of losing loved ones in the attack. For the families who lost a loved one, the impact was profound. The emotional devastation of knowing that a family member had been taken in such a violent and senseless way brought immeasurable grief and sorrow.

For those who survived, the trauma was no less significant. The shock and terror of the event left many feeling deeply unsettled, especially since the bombing was unexpected, occurring in what was supposed to be a joyful, celebratory setting—a concert. Many survivors reported ongoing struggles with flashbacks, panic attacks, and a fear of public places, particularly crowded environments. The long-term effects of such trauma extended far beyond the immediate aftermath, with both physical rehabilitation and emotional healing taking years.

In the years following the bombing, there were continued efforts to provide support for survivors and victims' families. Mental health resources became a focal point, with counseling and therapy services offered by local and national organizations. Charitable foundations were established, some of which were directly involved with the families affected by the tragedy. The We Love Manchester Emergency Fund, set up after the bombing, raised millions of pounds to provide immediate financial relief and support to those affected by the attack. This fund helped with medical expenses, funeral costs, and ongoing support for victims' families.

THE ROLE OF THE PUBLIC AND THE CITY OF MANCHESTER

In the hours and days following the bombing, the city of Manchester exhibited an extraordinary outpouring of support, unity, and resilience. Local residents, businesses, and organizations immediately began offering assistance. Blood donations were called for, and within hours, hundreds of people turned up at hospitals to donate blood. Businesses in the city opened their doors to help shelter those caught in the aftermath, offering food, shelter, and warmth. Taxi drivers provided free transportation to help people get home safely, while social media and community groups rallied together to offer support.

Manchester, known for its sense of community and collective spirit, quickly became a beacon of resilience in the face of terror. Despite the tragedy, the people of Manchester refused to let fear dictate their actions. Instead, they demonstrated that terrorism could not defeat their unity and determination. Manchester's official motto—"Concilio et Labore" ("By wisdom and effort")—was a fitting reflection of the city's response.

The aftermath of the bombing also saw the emergence of powerful public symbols, including the iconic bee symbol, which became a symbol of Manchester's strength and solidarity. The Manchester Bee, a historic emblem of the city representing its industriousness, was adopted by the public in a show of defiance against those who sought to instill fear. People wore bee tattoos, placed bee symbols on memorials, and displayed the bee on murals and art installations as a mark of remembrance for the victims and a symbol of the city's resilience.

THE ONE LOVE MANCHESTER CONCERT

One of the most significant and powerful responses to the bombing came in the form of the One Love Manchester benefit concert, which took place on June 4, 2017, less than two weeks after the attack. The concert was organized by Ariana Grande, the pop star whose concert was the target of the bombing, and aimed to raise funds for the victims and families affected by the tragedy. The event brought together an incredible lineup of artists, including Coldplay, Justin Bieber, Miley Cyrus, Niall Horan, Katy Perry, and many others, in a powerful display of solidarity and support for Manchester.

The concert took place at the Old Trafford Cricket Ground, with an audience of 50,000 people in attendance. The event raised over £17 million for the We Love Manchester Emergency Fund, which was used to support the victims and their families. It was a testament to the unifying power of music and how a community can come together in times of tragedy to show resilience, love, and hope. Ariana Grande, who was deeply affected by the bombing, was praised for her role in organizing the concert and for demonstrating her commitment to the Manchester community. The event also symbolized the refusal to let terrorism dictate the future and culture of the city.

The One Love Manchester concert was broadcast worldwide, allowing viewers from around the globe to participate in the show of support. It was a moment of healing for many and served as a direct challenge to the terrorists who sought to instill fear and division. The concert's message was clear: Love will always triumph over hate.

CHANGES IN COUNTERTERRORISM POLICY AND NATIONAL SECURITY

The Manchester Arena bombing had significant implications for national security and counterterrorism strategies in the United Kingdom. The attack raised questions about the UK's approach to radicalization and terrorism, particularly with regard to lone-wolf attacks and individuals radicalized within their own communities. Salman Abedi was able to carry out the attack despite previous intelligence warnings and surveillance that failed to prevent the attack. This prompted calls for reforms in how radicalization was monitored, how intelligence was shared, and how to prevent such attacks from happening in the future.

In the aftermath, the UK government placed increased emphasis on counter-radicalization initiatives and preventing extremism at a community level. The Prevent Strategy, which was already in place, was expanded to more effectively identify and support individuals at risk of radicalization, with the aim of intervening before they could act on extremist ideologies. Local authorities and schools began to focus more on educating young people about the dangers of radicalization and how to resist extremist ideologies.

At the same time, there were discussions about improving security at major public venues and events. In the wake of the Manchester Arena bombing, there was a push for more stringent security measures, such as bag checks, metal detectors, and an increased presence of security personnel at public venues. While some questioned whether such measures would infringe upon civil liberties, many felt that stronger security was necessary to deter future attacks.

Additionally, authorities began to explore ways to increase cooperation between countries and international organizations in combating terrorism. The international fight against terrorism was increasingly viewed as a collective responsibility that required nations to share intelligence and resources more effectively. Following the attack, cooperation between the UK and Libyan authorities intensified, as investigators sought to understand Abedi's connections to Libya and other extremist groups.

THE ROLE OF THE MEDIA AND PUBLIC PERCEPTION OF TERRORISM

The Manchester Arena bombing, like other terrorist attacks, underscored the role of the media in shaping public perception of terrorism. The media's coverage of the attack played a pivotal role in both spreading the news of the tragedy and in raising awareness of the broader issue of terrorism. While the attack was horrific, it also prompted global outpourings of support and solidarity for the victims and Manchester as a whole.

However, the media also played a role in fueling fear and anxiety about the threat of terrorism, which in turn affected public attitudes toward safety and security. News outlets, especially in the immediate aftermath, provided extensive coverage of the attack, with detailed reports on the explosion, the victims, and the investigation. While this was essential in informing the public, it also brought heightened attention to the risks of radicalization and terrorism in the modern world.

Many people, both within the UK and around the world, expressed concerns about the increasing frequency of such attacks, particularly in cities with large, diverse populations. For some, the Manchester bombing seemed to represent a new era of terrorism—one that was more personalized, radicalized from within, and difficult to predict or prevent. For others, it reinforced the importance of maintaining vigilance against extremist ideologies and understanding the complexities of modern terrorism.

A FINAL REFLECTION: STRENGTH IN THE FACE OF TERROR

In conclusion, the Manchester Arena bombing was a devastating and life-altering event that left an indelible mark on the city, the UK, and the global community. It was a senseless act of violence, targeted at innocent people, and it forever altered the lives of those affected. Yet, the aftermath of the attack revealed the resilience, strength, and unity of the people of Manchester and the wider public.

Despite the horror and tragedy of the bombing, the city of Manchester, as well as its residents and supporters around the world, refused to allow fear or hatred to define their response. In the face of terror, they chose love, solidarity, and healing. The events that followed the attack—from the One Love Manchester concert to the ongoing efforts of support and memorials for the victims—demonstrated the power of community in the face of unspeakable grief.

As the years pass, the legacy of the bombing continues to shape the conversation around terrorism, security, radicalization, and the importance of community solidarity. The Manchester Arena bombing serves as a reminder that, while terrorism can inflict immense suffering, the resilience of individuals and communities can overcome even the darkest of tragedies.

CHAPTER 7
THE ILLEGAL ADOPTION TRADE
FAMILY HEARTBREAK CONTINUES TODAY

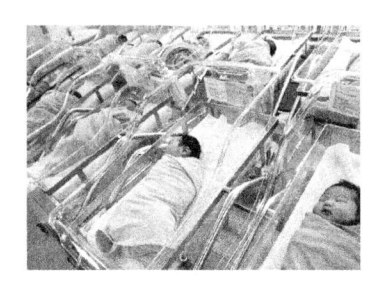

THE ROOTS OF THE ILLEGAL ADOPTION TRADE

The illegal adoption trade is an insidious and pervasive crime that has existed for centuries, exploiting vulnerable populations and circumventing the legal systems designed to protect children. This black market for children is driven by a complex combination of poverty, corruption, desperation, and greed, flourishing in countries with lax regulations, weak legal systems, or political instability. Understanding the origins of this illegal trade involves looking into the broader context of adoption itself, its historical evolution, and the numerous factors that have allowed this dark industry to take root and thrive in different parts of the world.

THE HISTORICAL FOUNDATIONS OF ADOPTION

Adoption as a practice has existed since ancient civilizations, although its role and purpose have evolved significantly over time. In early societies, adoption was often a legal means for securing inheritance or ensuring the continuity of a family line. It was typically used to bring children into wealthy or powerful families, often those without heirs. The concept of adopting for humanitarian reasons, such as providing a home for abandoned children or orphans, did not gain widespread traction until the late 19th and early 20th centuries.

As industrialization and urbanization increased in the West, so did the number of children who were orphaned or abandoned due to poverty, disease, and war. It was during this time that the modern notion of adoption began to take shape, with children being placed in homes not just to perpetuate family lines but to give them a better life. Yet, despite its noble intentions, the systems established for adoption began to reveal their vulnerabilities.

In the early 20th century, orphanages in Europe and the United States began to face overcrowding, as an increasing number of children were abandoned, and demand for adoption grew. This period of social upheaval and the aftermath of wars created fertile ground for the exploitation of children, leading to the emergence of the black market for adoption. In particular, children who were considered to be "surplus"—whether orphaned, abandoned, or born out of wedlock—became easy targets for criminals seeking to profit from the adoption process.

POST-WAR ERA: THE BEGINNINGS OF THE ILLEGAL ADOPTION TRADE

The roots of the modern illegal adoption trade can be traced to the aftermath of World War II, when millions of children in war-torn Europe were left orphaned or displaced. In countries such as Germany, Poland, and Italy, the need for homes for these children was critical. The global demand for adoptable children skyrocketed, and many found their way into the hands of people who sought to profit from the process.

One of the earliest and most well-known examples of this was the rise of international adoptions in the 1950s and 1960s. The United States, in particular, became a major destination for children from war-torn countries, as well as from countries experiencing political instability, such as Korea and later, Vietnam. While many of these adoptions were legitimate, a growing number of children were trafficked for adoption, either sold directly to adoptive families or routed through intermediary agencies that falsified documents.

In some countries, orphanages, adoption agencies, and even social workers participated in the illegal trade by fabricating birth records or convincing birth mothers to relinquish their children under false pretenses. These children, who were often born into poverty or from single mothers, were told that they were unfit to raise them or that their children would have a better life in another country. Some were coerced into signing away parental rights without understanding the full implications of their actions. Others were outright kidnapped from their biological families or removed from state care under false claims of abandonment.

THE RISE OF ADOPTION BROKERS AND TRAFFICKING RINGS

As the demand for adoptable children grew, so too did the market for illegal adoption. In the 1960s and 1970s, a more organized system began to emerge, with brokers acting as middlemen between birth mothers, orphanages, and adoptive families. These brokers, often operating through established adoption agencies or directly through hospitals and orphanages, played a crucial role in perpetuating the trade by facilitating the illegal transactions and creating false documentation to cover up the crimes.

These brokers were able to exploit weak legal systems and corruption within governments to make the trade easier. In some countries, officials were paid to overlook irregularities in the adoption process or to falsify records to make an adoption appear legal. In other cases, social workers and medical professionals actively participated in the trafficking process, facilitating the transfer of children across borders without any regard for their legal status.

One notorious example of such a trafficking operation occurred in the Philippines in the 1980s and 1990s, when children were abducted from poor families and placed for adoption with wealthy foreigners. Many children were trafficked to the United States and other Western nations, where they were sold to unsuspecting adoptive parents. While the scale of this operation was not widely known at the time, investigations later revealed that corrupt adoption agencies and officials were involved in falsifying birth certificates and legal documents to hide the truth from the authorities.

As international adoption gained popularity, the trafficking networks expanded. Children from countries such as Colombia, Guatemala, and Haiti were sent to the United States and Europe, where they were sold to wealthy families eager to adopt. These children were often taken under false pretenses—either through coercion, fraudulent birth certificates, or outright abductions. These criminal operations flourished in countries with limited oversight and weak regulatory frameworks governing adoption, where the demand for adoptable children outstripped the supply.

ECONOMIC AND SOCIAL FACTORS THAT FUEL THE TRADE

The growth of the illegal adoption trade can also be attributed to a number of economic and social factors that contribute to the vulnerability of children and their families. Poverty plays a major role in fueling illegal adoptions, particularly in developing nations. Many birth mothers, often single women, find themselves unable to care for their children due to lack of resources, housing, and social support. In some cases, they may be coerced or manipulated into giving up their children by adoption agencies or traffickers who promise them a better future for their child abroad.

In some countries, such as Ethiopia, India, and Cambodia, child abandonment is a result of cultural and societal pressures, including stigmatization of single mothers and the belief that a child born into poverty cannot have a future. These social pressures lead to high numbers of abandoned children, and traffickers take advantage of the lack of resources and infrastructure to create a black-market system for adoption.

Another factor that perpetuates the illegal adoption trade is the increasing demand for adoptive children in countries with more resources, such as the United States, Canada, and many European nations. The desire for children, particularly those who are young, healthy, and from certain ethnic backgrounds, fuels the trade. Adoption agencies in wealthier countries often work with intermediaries in poorer nations to facilitate the adoption process. While most of these agencies operate legally, some are complicit in the trafficking of children, either knowingly or unknowingly, by failing to thoroughly vet the origins of the children they place.

The promise of a better life in a foreign country is one of the most significant selling points for traffickers. Birth mothers, often living in desperate circumstances, are told that their children will be placed with loving families who can provide them with opportunities they cannot. For many, this seems like a noble sacrifice for their child's future, even though they are unaware that their child may be sold or trafficked into an illegal adoption system.

INTERNATIONAL LAWS AND LOOPHOLES

International agreements such as the 1993 Hague Convention on Protection of Children and Co-operation in Respect of Intercountry Adoption were designed to reduce the incidence of illegal adoptions and child trafficking. The Hague Convention sets standards for international adoption, aiming to protect children from being exploited or trafficked. However, the success of these measures has been limited, and enforcement remains a significant challenge.

One major issue is that not all countries are signatories to the Hague Convention, and some countries have not fully implemented or enforced the measures outlined in the agreement. Even in signatory countries, loopholes and a lack of effective enforcement allow the illegal trade to continue. The high demand for children in wealthier countries, coupled with the lack of comprehensive oversight in some of the sending countries, has created a situation in which criminal adoption rings continue to thrive.

THE CURRENT STATE OF THE ILLEGAL ADOPTION TRADE

The illegal adoption trade today operates globally, involving complex networks of corrupt government officials, adoption agencies, brokers, lawyers, and medical professionals who are willing to exploit vulnerable children and birth parents for financial gain. Despite efforts from governments, law enforcement agencies, and international organizations to curb illegal adoptions, the demand for children in developed nations fuels the market for child trafficking and exploitation. As a result, the trade remains widespread, especially in developing countries where children are often taken from poor families or orphanages, and their backgrounds are falsified to appear legal.

One of the major reasons the illegal adoption trade continues is the demand for children in wealthy countries. With increasing numbers of couples in the U.S., Europe, and other developed nations eager to adopt, and many legal adoption processes being long and expensive, traffickers and brokers exploit these desires. The existence of high fees for international adoptions in countries like the United States means there is a large financial incentive for illegal adoption networks to operate.

At the heart of the trade are the brokers and adoption agencies that facilitate the entire process, including the falsification of documents to make the illegal adoptions appear legitimate. These agencies work with corrupt officials—doctors, social workers, and sometimes law enforcement officers—to create fraudulent birth certificates, medical records, and other necessary documents that allow trafficked children to cross borders undetected.

HOW THE ILLEGAL ADOPTION TRADE OPERATES TODAY

The modern-day illegal adoption trade relies on several distinct methods to supply children to the market. While some of these methods are more covert, others are brazen in their manipulation of the legal adoption system.

DECEPTIVE PRACTICES AND EXPLOITATION OF BIRTH PARENTS

In many cases, children are sold into the adoption trade under the guise of legal adoption. Birth mothers in countries with high poverty levels are often approached by brokers or adoption agencies, who promise them financial assistance, medical care, or other forms of support. These women, often unaware of their legal rights or the long-term implications of their actions, are persuaded to relinquish their children.

In some countries, such as India and Guatemala, birth mothers are told that their children will be placed in a loving home in a foreign country and that their financial assistance will help improve their own lives. However, these mothers may not realize that their child is being trafficked into an illegal adoption market, and their consent may be coerced or obtained through deception. For example, birth mothers may be told that their children will receive better education or healthcare abroad, when in fact they are being sold for a significant sum to a foreign couple eager to adopt. In many cases, birth parents are unaware that they have been victims of a fraudulent scheme until much later, if at all.

Brokers often play a central role in connecting birth mothers with adopting parents. These intermediaries operate outside the legal system, gathering children from impoverished families or orphanages and pairing them with adoptive parents in wealthier nations. These brokers typically promise birth mothers financial compensation, a better life for their children, or assistance with their child's future, but their actions are far from transparent.

KIDNAPPING AND ABDUCTION

In addition to deceptive practices, child trafficking rings also resort to kidnapping and abduction as a means of obtaining children for illegal adoptions. In countries with unstable political climates or weak law enforcement, children are often abducted from hospitals, orphanages, and even from the streets. These abductions can be carried out by criminal organizations or corrupt individuals who have the power to bypass the legal system.

Children in poorer regions or those living in high-risk areas are particularly vulnerable to these crimes. Sometimes, children are taken from their families under false pretenses, such as being placed into foster care or given medical attention, only to be sold to adoption agencies or trafficked to foreign families. In some regions of Africa, Asia, and Central America, children are snatched from the streets or abducted from their homes by traffickers, with little hope of recovery for their families.

In the case of child abduction for adoption, the process often involves falsifying records and manipulating officials. Once a child is taken, their birth identity is erased or replaced with forged documents that allow them to be sold to adopting parents abroad. The children then disappear into the adoption system, where it becomes difficult to trace their origins or reunite them with their biological families.

CORRUPTION AND COLLUSION WITHIN ADOPTION AGENCIES

Corruption plays a significant role in facilitating illegal adoptions. In countries with weak legal frameworks or high levels of corruption, adoption agencies, social workers, and government officials may willingly or unknowingly be complicit in the illegal trade. For example, adoption agencies might deliberately circumvent the law by accepting bribes or falsifying documents to place children with foreign adoptive families, even when these children are not orphans, or their biological parents have not given proper consent.

In some instances, children may be taken from orphanages or medical facilities and transferred to private agencies or brokers, where they are illegally placed for adoption. This process often involves the forging of birth certificates, medical records, and other documentation to make the adoption appear legal. This is especially true in regions with limited oversight or where adoption laws are either outdated or poorly enforced.

The legal adoption process in some countries remains complex and slow, which leaves room for corruption. In Guatemala, for example, adoption was once known for being a high-risk area for illegal adoptions due to systemic corruption, and a significant number of children were trafficked for international adoption to the United States. Despite increased regulation, corruption within the adoption system continues to make it difficult to eliminate illegal adoptions altogether.

THE USE OF TECHNOLOGY AND ONLINE PLATFORMS

With the rise of the internet and social media, illegal adoption practices have adapted to the digital age. Brokers and traffickers are now using online platforms to connect adoptive parents with children in need of a home, bypassing official adoption channels. Online forums, social media groups, and websites dedicated to connecting birth mothers with prospective adoptive parents often operate in the gray area of the law, where it can be difficult to verify the legitimacy of the adoptions being arranged.

These online networks allow intermediaries to exploit both adoptive parents and birth mothers. In many cases, prospective parents search for children to adopt online, often because of long waiting periods or high costs associated with legitimate adoption agencies. While some of these transactions may be unintentional or based on misinformation, they can inadvertently contribute to the underground market of child trafficking. These platforms often serve as a conduit for brokers who facilitate illegal adoptions by matching children with parents, sometimes without full disclosure of the child's background or the legality of the process.

THE ROLE OF THE INTERNATIONAL COMMUNITY

While international conventions such as the Hague Convention on Protection of Children and Co-operation in Respect of Intercountry Adoption (1993) and the United Nations' Convention on the Rights of the Child (1989) have made significant strides in attempting to standardize adoption procedures and prevent illegal practices, the global nature of the adoption trade makes enforcement difficult. Corruption, bureaucratic inefficiency, and the sheer scale of the illegal adoption industry make it impossible to eliminate the trade entirely.

Many countries that participate in international adoption programs have implemented safeguards to protect against child trafficking, but implementation remains inconsistent. Some countries still do not have the legal frameworks or the resources necessary to regulate the adoption process adequately. In countries such as Ethiopia, Haiti, and Nepal, which are often among the most affected by the illegal adoption trade, widespread poverty, political instability, and a lack of oversight make it easier for traffickers to exploit vulnerable children.

Despite these challenges, there has been progress in improving international cooperation and developing standards for intercountry adoptions. The Hague Convention, for example, has made it more difficult for traffickers to place children in foreign homes without proper documentation, but much work remains to be done. More needs to be done to raise awareness among prospective adoptive parents about the risks of illegal adoptions and to strengthen the enforcement of international adoption laws.

THE IMPACT ON CHILDREN, BIRTH PARENTS, AND ADOPTIVE FAMILIES

The consequences of illegal adoption are far-reaching. For children, the consequences are often devastating. Many trafficked children grow up without knowledge of their true origins, facing identity crises and emotional distress. They may experience feelings of abandonment and confusion upon learning that they were trafficked for adoption, leading to lifelong psychological struggles. Additionally, these children are at risk of neglect, abuse, or exploitation in their new homes, as many trafficked children are sold into situations where they are poorly cared for or mistreated.

For birth parents, the pain of losing a child to trafficking is compounded by the lack of closure or the inability to reclaim their children. Many parents, especially in cases of abduction or deception, are never informed of the fate of their child, leaving them with unanswered questions and unresolved grief. The trauma of having a child stolen or sold under false pretenses can be unbearable for many birth mothers and fathers.

For adoptive families, the realization that they have unknowingly participated in an illegal adoption can be emotionally and financially devastating. Families may face legal battles, public scrutiny, and the emotional toll of discovering that their child was trafficked. In some cases, children are removed from adoptive homes if the adoption is discovered to be illegal, leaving both the child and the adoptive family broken.

CONCLUSION

The illegal adoption trade remains a persistent issue today, fueled by the high demand for children in wealthy countries, the corruption of officials, and the exploitation of vulnerable birth parents and children. Despite international efforts to combat trafficking and illegal adoptions, the trade continues to thrive in many parts of the world. Understanding the methods and consequences of this trade is crucial for raising awareness and creating effective solutions that protect children and families from exploitation. Only through increased regulation, international cooperation, and greater vigilance can we hope to put an end to this heartbreaking crime.

CHAPTER 8
THE EXXON VALDIZ OIL SPILL
ONE OF THE GREATEST MARINE DISASTERS IN HISTORY

Exxon Valdize

The Exxon Valdez oil spill is one of the most infamous environmental disasters in modern history. It occurred on March 24, 1989, when the Exxon Valdez, an oil tanker owned by the Exxon Corporation, struck a reef in Prince William Sound, Alaska. The incident resulted in the release of 10.8 million gallons of crude oil into the pristine waters of the sound, causing widespread devastation to the local marine and wildlife ecosystems. The spill's consequences were far-reaching and continue to impact environmental policy, corporate responsibility, and the ways in which oil spill management is approached.

BACKGROUND: THE EXXON VALDEZ AND PRINCE WILLIAM SOUND

Before the spill, the Exxon Valdez was considered one of the most advanced tankers in the world, with state-of-the-art technology designed to transport oil safely across the oceans. The ship, named after the Alaskan oil field where it loaded crude oil, was a single-hulled vessel that carried crude oil from Valdez, Alaska, to various ports on the West Coast of the United States.

Prince William Sound, where the spill occurred, is a vast and intricate system of bays, inlets, and islands. It is home to a diverse and vibrant ecosystem that includes rich marine life such as sea otters, harbor seals, and various species of fish, as well as migratory birds. The region is also vital for local communities who depend on fishing and tourism for their livelihoods. The sound's rugged coastline, with its numerous islands and coves, made it particularly vulnerable to oil spills, as the oil could easily become trapped in these narrow inlets, making cleanup efforts difficult and time-consuming.

THE DISASTER: THE SPILL OCCURS

On March 24, 1989, the Exxon Valdez was leaving the port of Valdez after loading up with crude oil. The tanker was heading out to sea, under the command of Captain Joseph Hazelwood, who was allegedly intoxicated at the time of the incident. The ship's navigational crew was also inexperienced, and it was later revealed that the ship was not equipped with a modern radar system, which could have potentially detected the reef and prevented the accident.

At approximately 12:04 a.m., the Exxon Valdez struck Bligh Reef, about 25 miles from the Valdez port. The collision caused the tanker's hull to rupture, releasing approximately 11 million gallons (about 257,000 barrels) of crude oil into the pristine waters of Prince William Sound. This was one of the largest oil spills in U.S. history at the time.

The damage was immediate and severe. The spilled oil quickly spread across the sound, covering thousands of miles of coastline, coating beaches, rocks, and marine life in its toxic residue. Within hours, the sound was transformed from a beautiful, vibrant ecosystem into a smothered and poisoned environment.

THE ENVIRONMENTAL IMPACT

The environmental impact of the Exxon Valdez oil spill was catastrophic. The crude oil that spilled into the waters of Prince William Sound was a mix of hydrocarbons, including benzene, toluene, and xylene, which are highly toxic to marine organisms. The oil coated the feathers of birds, fur of marine mammals, and the gills of fish, leading to the death of thousands of species.

Marine Life:

The spill decimated marine life in the sound. Sea otters, which rely on their fur for insulation against the cold waters, suffered terribly as their fur became coated with oil. The oil stripped the fur of its insulating properties, causing hypothermia in the otters, and many died from exposure. Approximately 2,800 sea otters were killed in the spill.

Similarly, harbor seals and other marine mammals were severely impacted. In total, estimates suggest that over 35,000 marine mammals were killed as a direct result of the spill.

The spill also had a significant impact on the fish populations in Prince William Sound. Many fish species, including salmon and herring, were exposed to toxic hydrocarbons. The eggs of these species were particularly vulnerable, as the oil contaminated their breeding grounds. Herring, in particular, suffered dramatic declines, which in turn impacted the larger food web that depended on them for sustenance.

Birds:

Birds, particularly seabirds, were among the most visible victims of the Exxon Valdez oil spill. An estimated 250,000 seabirds were killed as a result of the oil spill. The oil coated their feathers, causing them to lose buoyancy and insulation. Many birds died of hypothermia or were poisoned when they ingested the oil while trying to clean themselves. The loss of these birds was particularly tragic as many were migratory species, some of which had flown thousands of miles to reach their breeding grounds.

Plant Life:

The impact on plant life was also significant. The oil that washed ashore destroyed vast stretches of kelp forests and other marine vegetation. These ecosystems, which are important for providing shelter and food to a wide range of marine organisms, were severely damaged. The long-term impact of this loss was felt by the marine food chain, which was disrupted by the absence of these foundational species.

Coastal Ecosystems:

The oil spill caused severe damage to the coastal ecosystems of Prince William Sound. The intertidal zones, which are critical for a wide range of species, were smothered by oil, leading to the death of numerous invertebrates, shellfish, and other organisms that inhabit these areas. The loss of these species disrupted the entire coastal ecosystem.

The coastline itself was left scarred by the oil. Despite cleanup efforts, some areas of the coast remained contaminated with oil for years after the spill. The long-term environmental recovery of the sound has been slow, and some areas still show signs of damage.

THE RESPONSE: CLEANUP EFFORTS

The Exxon Valdez oil spill was a turning point in the way the U.S. approached oil spill response. Initially, Exxon and the federal government struggled to respond effectively to the disaster. The remote location of the spill, combined with the challenges of cleaning up oil in icy, turbulent waters, made the task seem almost insurmountable.

At first, the response was slow, and many experts criticized Exxon for its lack of preparation. The company's initial efforts were disorganized, and it was not until several days after the spill that a coordinated response effort began. Cleanup crews arrived in the region, using a combination of techniques, including mechanical skimmers, floating booms to contain the oil, and chemical dispersants to break up the oil. However, many of these techniques were ineffective in the harsh Alaskan environment, where the oil was quickly trapped in narrow coves and icy waters.

One of the most controversial aspects of the response was the use of chemical dispersants, which were sprayed over the oil to break it into smaller droplets. While this made the oil less visible on the surface, it did little to reduce the toxic impact on marine life. The dispersants caused the oil to sink, leading to contamination of the sea floor, where it persisted for years.

Despite the best efforts of cleanup teams, the oil spill's long-term environmental effects continued to unfold. The full recovery of the ecosystem would take decades, and some species are still struggling to return to pre-spill population levels.

LEGAL AND FINANCIAL AFTERMATH

In the aftermath of the Exxon Valdez spill, a complex legal battle ensued. Exxon was initially sued by the federal government, as well as by state and local entities, for the environmental damages caused by the spill. The company was held liable for the spill and was required to pay millions of dollars in damages and fines.

The legal process was long and complicated, and in 1994, Exxon and the federal government reached a settlement. Exxon was ordered to pay $900 million for the cleanup and restoration efforts, and in 1996, it was further ordered to pay an additional $5 billion in punitive damages.

However, the legal battle did not end there. The issue of punitive damages was contested, and in 2008, the U.S. Supreme Court reduced the amount of punitive damages to $507 million. Exxon's reluctance to fully compensate the affected communities and the environment led to ongoing resentment and criticism of the company.

In addition to the legal battles, the spill had a significant economic impact on the region. The local fishing industry, which was heavily dependent on the clean waters of Prince William Sound, suffered severe losses in the years following the spill. The fishing industry was not the only one impacted by the disaster. The tourism industry also took a hit, as the pristine beauty of the region was overshadowed by the environmental damage.

THE LONG-TERM EFFECTS AND RECOVERY

The Exxon Valdez oil spill left an indelible mark on the environment of Prince William Sound and Alaska as a whole. While some species have managed to recover over time, others have not. The long-term environmental effects continue to be studied, and some of the damage is still visible to this day. Oil continues to seep from the sea floor in some areas, and the full ecological recovery is still an ongoing process.

The oil spill also led to major changes in environmental policy. In response to the spill, the U.S. government passed the Oil Pollution Act of 1990, which established stricter regulations for the oil industry and improved the federal government's ability to respond to oil spills. The law required companies to have contingency plans in place for dealing with oil spills and mandated that tankers be double-hulled, which would reduce the risk of a similar disaster occurring in the future.

LEGACY OF THE EXXON VALDEZ OIL SPILL

The Exxon Valdez oil spill is a stark reminder of the environmental risks associated with the oil industry. It is also a story of corporate negligence, environmental destruction, and the long, arduous process of recovery. The tragedy demonstrated how a single accident could devastate an entire ecosystem and the livelihoods of countless people.

The spill changed the way we think about oil and the environment. It highlighted the need for stronger regulations, more effective cleanup methods, and greater corporate accountability. Although the ecosystems of Prince William Sound are slowly recovering, the long-lasting consequences of the Exxon Valdez oil spill serve as a warning for future generations about the dangers of oil extraction and the importance of safeguarding the environment.

CHAPTER 9
JEFFREY EPSTEIN
MASTER OF DEPRAVITY

Jeffrey Epstein

Jeffrey Epstein, born on January 20, 1953, in Brooklyn, New York, is perhaps one of the most controversial and enigmatic figures of the 21st century. His rise to wealth, influence, and infamy remains a subject of intrigue and speculation. Epstein's life story, particularly his early years and ascent to the financial elite, is marked by ambiguity, opportunism, and an ability to build connections with some of the most powerful people in the world. To understand how Epstein became a multi-millionaire and gained access to the circles of wealth, politics, and power, it's essential to explore his formative years, early career, and the relationships that helped propel his rise.

EARLY LIFE

Epstein was born into a working-class family in Brooklyn, New York, to parents Seymour and Pauline Epstein. Seymour Epstein worked as a groundskeeper in the city, while Pauline was a homemaker. Epstein's upbringing was modest, and his family's financial status was far from affluent. The Epsteins lived in the Coney Island area of Brooklyn, a neighborhood that was home to a diverse population but far removed from the glamorous wealth and elite circles Epstein would later navigate.

Epstein attended John Dewey High School in Brooklyn, where he was known to be a bright student, though not particularly exceptional in terms of grades. Nevertheless, he had a charisma and charm that made him stand out among his peers. It's said that Epstein was highly ambitious from a young age and understood the value of making connections with influential people. His early life was marked by an unusual mix of intellectual curiosity and a desire to engage with those in positions of power, a trait that would later define his career.

After graduating high school, Epstein enrolled at CUNY (City University of New York), where he studied physics and mathematics. His academic career was not particularly distinguished, and he graduated without earning a degree, which led him to teach briefly at the Dalton School, an elite private school in Manhattan. Epstein's time as a teacher was short-lived, and it was here that his rise to wealth and influence would take a critical turn. Epstein's ability to ingratiate himself with influential figures during this period helped lay the groundwork for his future success.

At Dalton, Epstein taught math and physics, but his real talents seemed to lie in networking. He quickly became friends with the school's headmaster, Donald Barr, who was the father of William Barr, later U.S. Attorney General. Donald Barr was a former CIA officer, which would prove to be a significant connection for Epstein in the years to come. His rapport with Barr would later lead to an introduction to key figures in the financial world, marking the beginning of Epstein's transition into the world of high finance.

ENTRY INTO THE WORLD OF FINANCE

Epstein's first major step into the world of finance came when he was hired by Bear Stearns, an investment bank, in the mid-1970s. Although his official job title was that of a junior assistant, it is widely believed that Epstein quickly made a name for himself as someone with an uncanny ability to deal with wealthy clients. His time at Bear Stearns marked the beginning of his ascent to the upper echelons of the financial world, though the specifics of his responsibilities and the nature of his early work are largely shrouded in mystery. Epstein was known to be involved in handling high-net-worth individuals and was skilled at working with complex financial strategies that allowed the wealthy to avoid taxes and other regulatory constraints.

Epstein's early success in finance is often attributed to his charm and ability to connect with powerful individuals. He was particularly adept at dealing with those who had amassed considerable fortunes and were looking for ways to protect their wealth. Epstein's skillset included managing investments, dealing with trusts, and offering exclusive services to the elite. Though he had no formal background in finance beyond his time at Bear Stearns, Epstein's ability to network and understand the intricate needs of the ultra-wealthy helped him stand out.

KEY RELATIONSHIPS AND THE RISE TO WEALTH

Epstein's connections with powerful individuals were the linchpin of his rise to millionaire status. One of the most significant relationships he formed was with Leslie Wexner, the billionaire founder of L Brands, the company behind Victoria's Secret and other popular brands. Wexner would become one of Epstein's most important clients and mentors, with their business relationship transforming into a deep financial and personal connection.

Epstein's work with Wexner is perhaps the most mysterious and crucial aspect of his rise to wealth. By the 1980s, Epstein had gained the trust of Wexner, and Epstein became the primary financial manager for Wexner's vast wealth. Epstein was given control over Wexner's personal finances, including his real estate holdings, investments, and charitable foundations. Wexner entrusted Epstein with managing his finances to such an extent that Epstein had near total control over many of Wexner's business and personal decisions. It was during this period that Epstein's wealth truly began to accumulate.

The relationship between Epstein and Wexner raised eyebrows for its unusual nature. Epstein reportedly had access to Wexner's private properties, including a mansion in New York, and his influence over Wexner's finances was substantial. The specifics of their financial arrangements remain murky, but it's clear that Epstein leveraged his role with Wexner to gain access to other high-net-worth individuals and to build his own wealth.

Epstein also cultivated relationships with other influential figures, including former presidents, royalty, academics, and business magnates. His social network included people like Bill Clinton, Donald Trump, Prince Andrew, and Alan Dershowitz, among others. These connections allowed Epstein to maintain an aura of power and respectability, even as his financial dealings and personal life raised questions. Epstein was known for hosting lavish parties on his private jet, the "Lolita Express," and on his private island, Little Saint James in the U.S. Virgin Islands. These gatherings were attended by celebrities, politicians, and business leaders, further cementing his position within the circles of wealth and power.

Despite his success, Epstein's wealth remained somewhat opaque. He was not a publicly listed figure in the traditional sense, and many questioned how he made his fortune. While he was known for managing the wealth of the ultra-rich, there were few details available about how Epstein personally made his money. This secrecy surrounding his financial dealings, combined with his ability to attract powerful individuals, added to the mystery of his wealth and influence.

EPSTEIN'S PERSONAL LIFE AND HIS PATH TO INFAMY

By the late 1990s and early 2000s, Epstein had transformed into a figure who was not only financially successful but also known for his controversial personal life. He was rumored to be involved in various illicit activities, including running a sex trafficking operation, but these allegations did not surface publicly until much later. Epstein's wealth, however, seemed secure, bolstered by his ability to maintain strong relationships with influential figures and by his mysterious and lucrative financial dealings.

Epstein's rise to millionaire status was, in many ways, a product of his personal connections and his ability to tap into the networks of the wealthy elite. His story is one of ambition, manipulation, and strategic alliances, though it ultimately became overshadowed by criminal activity and scandal.

THE EARLY ALLEGATIONS AND FIRST CONVICTION

Jeffrey Epstein's criminal activities didn't come to public attention overnight. In fact, his sexual abuse of minors and other illegal activities began years before his first legal troubles. In the early 2000s, Epstein was known for his lavish lifestyle, which included private islands, luxury jets, and a network of high-profile friends and acquaintances. However, beneath this facade of wealth and influence, Epstein was operating a criminal enterprise of sexual abuse and exploitation.

The first major public legal issue Epstein faced was in 2005, when a woman reported to the Palm Beach, Florida, police that her 14-year-old stepdaughter had been sexually abused by Epstein. This prompted an investigation into Epstein's activities, leading to further allegations. In 2006, the Palm Beach police department began gathering evidence that Epstein was running an extensive operation in which underage girls were sexually exploited and trafficked. Multiple women came forward to accuse Epstein of abusing them, often after being recruited under the guise of giving massages.

These allegations led to a grand jury investigation, but Epstein's wealth and connections allowed him to avoid serious legal consequences at that time. In 2008, Epstein struck a controversial plea deal with federal prosecutors that would have far-reaching implications for his future. He pleaded guilty to one count of soliciting prostitution from a minor, a charge that carried a sentence of only 18 months in prison. This plea deal, known as the "non-prosecution agreement" (NPA), was signed in secret and allowed Epstein to avoid federal charges for sex trafficking minors. Epstein served only 13 months in a county jail, with many privileges that were not typically granted to other inmates, including being allowed to leave the jail during the day for "work release" purposes.

The deal was widely criticized, with many arguing that it was a result of Epstein's wealth, influence, and connections, and that it protected powerful individuals who may have been involved in his criminal enterprise. The leniency of Epstein's sentence, combined with the secrecy surrounding the deal, sparked public outrage, especially among the women who had accused him of abuse. Despite the light sentence, Epstein was still legally required to register as a sex offender, but he was allowed to continue his life as a relatively free man, allowing him to expand his network of abuse further.

THE EXPANSION OF EPSTEIN'S CRIMES

Epstein's activities were far from limited to the events in Palm Beach, Florida. In the years following his conviction, Epstein continued to exploit young women and minors on a global scale. He was known for traveling frequently to his private island, Little Saint James, in the U.S. Virgin Islands, where he allegedly ran his sex trafficking operation. Epstein's private island was reported to be the central hub of his criminal activities, but it was not the only location where he preyed on young women and girls. He had multiple properties, including mansions in New York, New Mexico, and Paris, which were used to house and abuse young women, some of whom were reportedly under the age of 16.

Epstein's modus operandi involved recruiting vulnerable young girls, often from poor backgrounds or those facing difficult circumstances. Many of his victims were recruited under the pretense of earning money through modeling or as masseuses. These young women were often lured to Epstein's properties with promises of money, and once there, they were coerced into sexual acts. These abuses were often perpetrated in front of Epstein and other powerful individuals, some of whom reportedly participated in or were complicit in the exploitation.

GHISLAINE MAXWELL :- WILLING ACCOMPLICE

Jeffrey Epstein's relationship with Ghislaine Maxwell is one of the most pivotal and controversial aspects of his criminal activities. The two were closely connected for many years, with their bond playing a central role in the operations of Epstein's sex trafficking ring. Maxwell, a British socialite and daughter of the late media mogul Robert Maxwell, was deeply embedded in Epstein's world, and her role has been the subject of intense scrutiny. Their relationship was not only personal but also professional, as Maxwell was alleged to have played a key role in recruiting, grooming, and trafficking young women for Epstein's sexual abuse.

PERSONAL AND PROFESSIONAL RELATIONSHIP

Epstein and Maxwell's relationship was multi-faceted, with both personal and business elements intertwined. They met in the early 1990s, and Maxwell quickly became a prominent figure in Epstein's life. At the time, she was in her late 20s and already well-connected in elite social circles, due in part to her father's vast wealth and influence. It was through these circles that she and Epstein initially became acquainted.

Maxwell was known for her charm, wit, and social skills, qualities that made her an effective partner in Epstein's operations. Over time, she became his confidante, and the two were often seen together at high-profile events. Their friendship appeared close, but as time went on, their relationship evolved into something far more complicated and sinister.

Epstein and Maxwell were often seen together at his properties, including Little Saint James, his mansion in New York, and other locations that were central to his trafficking activities. Many of Epstein's victims have accused Maxwell of recruiting them, often under false pretenses, such as offering money or opportunities for modeling. Maxwell allegedly played a key role in the process of grooming young girls for Epstein, building their trust, and preparing them for sexual exploitation.

ROLE IN EPSTEIN'S SEX TRAFFICKING OPERATION

Maxwell's involvement in Epstein's criminal enterprise was extensive. She was not just a passive accomplice; she was an active participant in the abuse and trafficking of young women. Several survivors have testified that Maxwell would often approach them with offers of work, such as modeling or giving massages, and would introduce them to Epstein. Once they were brought into his world, Maxwell would act as an intermediary, facilitating their introduction to Epstein and sometimes directly participating in the abuse.

Her role was crucial in maintaining the operation. Maxwell was reportedly responsible for managing and recruiting the girls who were trafficked to Epstein's private estates. She helped create a network of women, many of whom were vulnerable, poor, or coming from troubled backgrounds, making them easy targets for Epstein and his associates. Maxwell was also believed to have been involved in organizing Epstein's infamous parties and gatherings, where abuse was often carried out.

While Epstein used his wealth and power to manipulate and intimidate, Maxwell leveraged her social status and charm to gain access to potential victims. Her background, as the daughter of Robert Maxwell, gave her the ability to navigate elite circles and provided her with the resources to lure girls into Epstein's web. Her connections also helped her gain entry to some of the highest echelons of society, including relationships with prominent figures in politics, business, and the entertainment world.

In addition to his abuse of underage girls, Epstein allegedly trafficked these young women to his friends and acquaintances, many of whom were high-profile figures from various sectors, including business, entertainment, and politics. Some of the names that have been associated with Epstein's criminal network include former U.S. Presidents Bill Clinton and Donald Trump, Prince Andrew of the British royal family, and well-known figures like Alan Dershowitz and Les Wexner. However, many of these associations remain speculative, and while some have denied any wrongdoing, the links between Epstein and such powerful figures have only fueled conspiracy theories and public speculation.

The nature of Epstein's operation was not limited to exploiting young women. Reports suggest that he created a system to maintain control over his victims. Epstein allegedly used manipulation, blackmail, and threats to keep his victims silent and compliant. Some women have claimed that they were forced into a system of silence through intimidation and fear of retribution. Epstein's power and influence allowed him to remain shielded from significant legal consequences for many years, despite mounting evidence of his criminal behavior.

2019 ARREST AND CHARGES

Epstein's arrest in July 2019 marked a significant turning point in the public's understanding of his crimes. After years of legal maneuvering and multiple investigations, Epstein was finally taken into custody on federal charges of sex trafficking minors. He was accused of operating an extensive criminal enterprise that exploited girls as young as 14 for sex, while using his vast network of wealth and power to shield himself from prosecution.

Epstein's arrest came on the heels of a Miami Herald investigation, which brought attention to the secrecy of his 2008 plea deal and the numerous women who had been victimized by Epstein over the years. The investigation prompted renewed interest in Epstein's activities, and soon after, a federal grand jury indicted him on sex trafficking charges.

The federal indictment painted a disturbing picture of Epstein's operation, accusing him of recruiting underage girls for sex and exploiting them at his various properties. It also alleged that Epstein had used his vast wealth and influence to intimidate and silence witnesses, furthering his ability to operate without legal repercussions. The indictment cited numerous victims, some of whom came forward to testify against Epstein, recounting the horrific abuse they endured at his hands.

Epstein's arrest, however, was met with another tragic twist. In August 2019, Epstein was found dead in his cell at the Metropolitan Correctional Center (MCC) in New York, where he was awaiting trial. The official cause of death was ruled a suicide by hanging, but the circumstances surrounding his death have raised numerous questions and conspiracy theories mainly due to his extensive relationships with noted people. Epstein's death, just weeks after his arrest, sparked widespread disbelief and led to speculations that he may have been murdered to prevent him from implicating others in his criminal network.

Many have questioned how Epstein, a high-profile prisoner with a history of suicide attempts and close surveillance, was able to die under such questionable circumstances. His death has been the subject of numerous conspiracy theories, with some speculating that powerful figures were involved in orchestrating his death to protect themselves from the fallout of the investigation.

THE IMPACT OF EPSTEIN'S CRIMES

The fallout from Epstein's crimes has been far-reaching, with countless women coming forward to recount their abuse and demand justice. His case has highlighted the ways in which the wealthy and powerful can use their influence to evade justice, and how victims of sexual abuse can be silenced for years. Epstein's criminal activities exposed the dark underbelly of power, wealth, and privilege, raising serious questions about how sexual exploitation can be hidden within the circles of the rich and powerful.

Epstein's case has also drawn attention to the issue of sex trafficking, particularly the trafficking of minors. His crimes have served as a stark reminder of the vulnerability of young women and the predators who exploit them. In the wake of his arrest, various investigations have been launched to uncover the full extent of his operations, and there is still much to learn about the scope of his criminal network.

Additionally, the connections Epstein had with powerful figures have left a lasting stain on many high-profile individuals, who now face questions about their knowledge of Epstein's activities and their potential involvement in his network of abuse.

MAXWELL FINALLY FACES CONSEQUENCES

Maxwell's role in Epstein's crimes became widely known after Epstein's arrest in 2019. Following Epstein's death in August 2019, Maxwell became a central figure in investigations into the sex trafficking operation. She was arrested in July 2020 and charged with multiple offenses, including sex trafficking of minors, conspiracy to entice minors to engage in illegal sex acts, and perjury. The charges were related to her alleged role in recruiting and grooming girls for Epstein, as well as her participation in the sexual abuse and exploitation.

Maxwell's trial began in late 2021, and it marked a significant moment in the pursuit of justice for Epstein's victims. Throughout the trial, Maxwell faced accusations from multiple women who alleged that she had not only helped Epstein in their abuse but had actively participated in the exploitation. Maxwell denied all charges, claiming that she was being scapegoated for Epstein's actions. Found guilty on all charges Maxwell was sentenced to 20 years in prison.

CONCLUSION

Jeffrey Epstein's criminal activities were not merely the actions of an individual. They were part of a much larger system of abuse, manipulation, and exploitation that spanned decades and affected countless victims. Epstein's ability to evade justice for so long was a result of his wealth and connections. When his crimes finally caught up with hime he saw suicide as the only option leaving a mass of unanswered questions about the identities of those involved in his horrendous crimes. Time will tell whether they too will face justice in the future.

CHAPTER 10
THE 2002 BALI BOMBINGS
BRUTAL ATTACKS ON NIGHTCLUB REVELLERS

Bali Bombing Memorial

The 2002 Bali bombings, which took place on October 12, 2002, are remembered as one of the deadliest and most traumatic terrorist attacks in Southeast Asia, as well as one of the most devastating terrorist attacks in modern history. The bombings, which targeted two popular nightclubs in the tourist-heavy district of Kuta on the island of Bali, Indonesia, were carried out by a network of extremists with connections to Al-Qaeda and were aimed at both killing civilians and making a powerful political statement against Western interests.

This chapter delves into the background of the attack, the perpetrators, the execution of the bombing, the immediate aftermath, the global and local reactions, and the long-lasting impact of the tragedy on Bali, Indonesia, and the world. We will also explore the implications of the attack in the context of global terrorism, Indonesia's security challenges, and the broader fight against extremism.

INTRODUCTION TO BALI AND THE CONTEXT OF THE ATTACK

Bali, an island province of Indonesia, has long been a popular tourist destination, known for its tropical climate, beautiful beaches, rich cultural heritage, and vibrant tourism industry. The island attracts millions of international tourists annually, making tourism a major contributor to Indonesia's economy. By the early 2000s, Bali had become one of the most sought-after destinations in Southeast Asia.

In the years preceding the 2002 bombings, however, Indonesia had faced growing political instability and security concerns, particularly in the wake of the 1998 Asian financial crisis and the subsequent fall of President Suharto's regime. Indonesia's transition to democracy, as well as regional separatist movements and religious tensions, provided fertile ground for extremist ideologies to take root. At the same time, the global threat of terrorism, particularly following the 9/11 attacks in the United States, led to increased concerns about radicalization and the spread of Islamic extremism.

In this context, Bali, as a key tourism hub and symbol of the thriving Indonesian economy, became a prime target for terrorist groups seeking to strike at Western interests and to show their strength in a region that had experienced increasing political instability. While the attackers' motivations were complex and rooted in a broader agenda, the bombings were a direct response to the rise of Western influence in Indonesia and to the Indonesian government's cooperation with the global war on terror.

THE ROLE OF JEMAAH ISLAMIYAH AND AL-QAEDA

The 2002 Bali bombings were perpetrated by Jemaah Islamiyah (JI), an Islamist extremist group with connections to Al-Qaeda. JI was founded in the 1990s by radical Islamist clerics and militants in Southeast Asia. It was initially established with the aim of creating a pan-Islamic state in Southeast Asia, incorporating Indonesia, the Philippines, Malaysia, and Brunei, as well as parts of southern Thailand and Myanmar. The group's ideology was rooted in a strict interpretation of Islam, which viewed secular governments and Western influences as corrupting forces that needed to be eliminated.

JI was inspired by the global jihadist movement and had strong ties to Al-Qaeda, particularly after the September 11, 2001, attacks in the United States. The group's leaders were motivated by a desire to wage violent jihad against perceived enemies of Islam, including the U.S., Western nations, and local governments that cooperated with the West. The Bali bombings were part of a broader strategy by JI to target soft Western targets in Southeast Asia, sending a message that the region was not immune to the global struggle against Western imperialism and secularism.

THE ROLE OF AL-QAEDA

Al-Qaeda, the global jihadist group led by Osama bin Laden, played a significant role in the ideological and operational support for Jemaah Islamiyah. Though Al-Qaeda did not directly plan or carry out the Bali bombings, the attack was aligned with the broader goals of the Al-Qaeda network. Al-Qaeda's support for jihadist organizations in Southeast Asia, including JI, was part of its broader strategy to promote global Islamic extremism and to establish an international network of radical militants willing to carry out acts of terrorism.

Al-Qaeda's connection to JI was also logistical. The 2002 Bali bombing plot involved the use of explosives and tactics that mirrored those used in other Al-Qaeda operations. The bombings were carried out in a manner designed to cause maximum destruction and to kill as many civilians as possible. The use of large, powerful bombs and the targeting of places with high numbers of Westerners were consistent with Al-Qaeda's modus operandi, as the group sought to weaken global powers by attacking their citizens abroad.

THE EXECUTION OF THE BALI BOMBINGS : PLANNING

The planning of the Bali bombings involved a network of JI militants working with other regional Islamist extremists. The mastermind behind the attack was Riduan Isamuddin, better known as Hambali, who was a senior member of Jemaah Islamiyah and a key figure in the Southeast Asian jihadist movement. Hambali was believed to have received training from Al-Qaeda and had close connections with the group's leadership. He was instrumental in facilitating the training, planning, and execution of the attack.

The bombing plan was meticulously coordinated. A group of JI militants, including the bombers themselves, travelled to Bali in the months leading up to the attack, conducting surveillance on popular tourist spots, gathering intelligence, and procuring materials for the bombs. The plan involved using multiple bombings at different locations to maximize casualties and impact. Bali's Kuta district, known for its vibrant nightlife and Western tourists, was chosen as the prime target.

The main bombing took place at the Sari Club, a popular nightclub located in the heart of Kuta, where large numbers of tourists gathered each night. The attackers also targeted the nearby Paddy's Pub, another club frequented by Westerners. The attackers placed the bombs in rented vans, which were then parked outside the clubs. The vans were loaded with a large quantity of explosives and set to detonate at specific times.

On the evening of October 12, 2002, the first bomb exploded outside the Sari Club, killing and injuring dozens of people. Moments later, a second, much larger bomb went off near Paddy's Pub, resulting in a much higher number of casualties. The massive explosions were followed by fires, chaos, and confusion. People who had been enjoying the nightlife were caught in a deadly inferno as the bombs ripped through the area.

In addition to the main bombings, a third smaller bomb was set off in the nearby neighborhood of Jimbaran Bay, targeting a convoy of police officers. While this attack was less deadly, it was part of the same coordinated campaign of violence aimed at terrorizing the population.

THE IMPACT OF THE BOMBINGS

The Bali bombings were devastating. Over 200 people were killed, and more than 200 others were injured, many of them critically. The majority of the victims were foreigners, with Australians being the most significant group among the dead and injured. However, many Indonesians were also among the casualties, including security personnel, workers at the nightclubs, and bystanders.

The immediate impact of the attack was profound. The explosion created massive destruction in the surrounding area, leaving buildings and streets in ruins. The bombings caused not only physical destruction but also psychological trauma. For the survivors, many of whom were seriously injured, the attack was a life-altering experience that left deep emotional and physical scars.

The attack sent shockwaves through Bali's tourism industry, which had been one of the most important economic sectors in the region. Bali's reputation as a safe and idyllic holiday destination was shattered, and tourism numbers plummeted in the immediate aftermath of the bombings. Many tourists were frightened away by the possibility of further attacks, and businesses in the affected areas saw a dramatic decline in revenue.

In the weeks and months following the attack, Bali's recovery was slow. The government and local community worked to rebuild the physical infrastructure, but the psychological and economic damage was more difficult to heal. The bombings had a lasting effect on the social and political landscape of Bali, Indonesia, and the broader Southeast Asian region.

THE GLOBAL AND LOCAL REACTIONS : INTERNATIONAL RESPONSE

The international response to the Bali bombings was swift and overwhelmingly condemning. World leaders expressed their shock and solidarity with Indonesia, sending messages of support to the victims and their families. The Australian government, in particular, was deeply affected by the attack, as many of the victims were Australian nationals. The Australian government vowed to bring those responsible for the bombings to justice, and it played a crucial role in the subsequent investigation and intelligence-sharing efforts.

The bombings also led to a renewed focus on global terrorism, especially in Southeast Asia. Many countries, including the United States, Australia, and the United Kingdom, pledged to assist Indonesia in strengthening its counterterrorism capabilities. This marked a significant shift in international cooperation, as countries recognized the need to work together to combat the growing threat of Islamist extremism in the region.

LOCAL RESPONSE

Locally, the reaction to the Bali bombings was marked by grief, confusion, and anger. Indonesians were shocked by the scale of the attack, which had claimed so many lives, and many expressed their horror that their beloved island of Bali had become the site of such a violent act. For the Indonesian government, the attack posed serious security and political challenges, as the bombing was seen as an affront to the country's tourism-based economy, as well as an attack on its international image.

In Bali itself, survivors, their families, and the broader community came together in the aftermath of the tragedy to support one another. Religious and community leaders in Bali and throughout Indonesia organized memorial services, vigils, and other events to honor the victims. These events were also used to promote messages of peace and reconciliation, countering the hatred and violence that had been perpetuated by the terrorists.

INVESTIGATION

The organization suspected of responsibility for the bombing was Jemaah Islamiya an Islamist group allegedly led by radical cleric Abu Bakar Bashir. A week after the blasts, Arab satellite channel Al Jazeera put to air an audio cassette purportedly carrying a recorded voice message from Osama Bin Laden that stated the Bali bombings were in direct retaliation for support of the United States' war on Terror and Australia's role in the liberation of Timor-Leste.

You will be killed just as you kill, and will be bombed just as you bomb. Expect more that will further distress you.

The recording did not however claim responsibility for the Bali attack. Former FBI agent Ali Soufan confirmed in his book, *The Black Banners*, that al-Qaeda did in fact finance the attack. In addition, Riduan Isamuddin confessed that al-Qaeda had sent him US$30,000 to fund the bombings of the two nightclubs.

Aris Munandar (aka Sheik Aris) is a Jemaah Islamiyah associate linked to Bashir. He is believed to have assisted the Bali bomber Amrozi in acquiring some of the explosives used in the Bali bombings. Philippine intelligence considers Munandar to be associated with Mohammad Abdullah Sughayer, a

Saudi national Abu Sayyaf Group in southern Philippines. Munandar is still at large. A report by the United States-Indonesia Society describes the arrest of Amrozi and other suspects.

General Pastika ordered his men to make the arrest early the next morning, November. Amrozi was asleep in the rear of the house. According to Greg Barton's account, Amrozi did not attempt to escape, but laughed instead, later exclaiming, "Gosh, you guys are very clever, how did you find me?" Amrozi's mobile phone, a particularly important piece of evidence, was seized during his arrest. Bags of chemical ingredients for bombs were found in his workshop and soil samples aken from outside his home showed traces of the primary chemical used in the Sari Club bomb. Police found receipts or the purchase of chemicals used to make the bombs, as well as a list of expenses incurred in making the bombs. Further search of Amrozi's home revealed copies of speeches by Osama bin Laden, and Abu Bakar Bashir, the radical Indonesian Muslim cleric reputed to be the leader of Jemaah Islamiyah. The speeches exhorted listeners to wage. Police also uncovered training manuals on ambush techniques and numerous articles on jihad. Under questioning Amrozi revealed the names of six others involved in the bombing: Ali Imron, Imam Samudra, Dul Matin, Idris, Abdul Ghani and Umar Patek. But Amrozi's mobile phone proved to be the real catch. Indonesian investigators were able to print out a list of calls he had made immediately before, during and after the bombing, as well as the names and telephone numbers in the phone's memory. Pastika kept Amrozi's arrest secret for two days. After it was announced, Polri monitored the sudden flurry of communications among numbers listed in Amrozi's telephone before the calls abruptly ceased. The investigators were able to identify the location of a number of the telephones, leading to a series of arrests.

Indonesian authorities also believe more suspects remain at large. In 2005, Indonesian police arrested 24 additional people suspected of involvement in the Bali attacks and a 2003 bombing of the Marriott Hotel in Jakarta.

On 12 October 2005, a story in Australian broadcaster SBS's documentary series *Dateline*, called "Inside Indonesia's War on Terrorism", argued that the Indonesian military or police may have been involved in executing the attack.

On 13 June 2007, it was reported that Abu Dujana, who might have headed a terrorist cell in Bali, was captured.

INITIAL CHARGES AND TRIALS

In April 2003, Indonesian authorities charged Abu Bakar Bashir (also rendered "Ba'asyir"), the alleged spiritual leader of Jemaah Islamiyah, with treason. It was alleged that he tried to overthrow the government and establish an Islamic state. The specific charges against Bashir related to a series of church bombings on Christmas Eve in 2000, and to a plot to bomb United States and other Western interests in Singapore. He was initially not charged over the Bali attack, although he was frequently accused of being the instigator or inspirer of the attack. On 2 September, Bashir was acquitted of treason but convicted of lesser charges and sentenced to a prison term of four years. He said he would appeal.

On 15 October 2004, he was arrested by the Indonesian authorities and charged with involvement in another bomb attack, which killed 14 people at the J. W. Marriott hotel in Jakarta on 5 August 2003. Secondary charges in this indictment accused him of involvement in the Bali bombing, the first time he faced charges in relation to this attack.

On 3 March 2005, Bashir was found not guilty of the charges surrounding the 2003 bombing, but guilty of conspiracy over the 2002 attacks in Bali. He was sentenced to two and a half years imprisonment. The Australian, US, and many governments expressed its disappointment that the sentence was too short. In the outcome, Bashir was freed on 14 June 2006 having served less than 26 months for his conspiracy. On 21 December 2006, Bashir's conviction was overturned by Indonesia's Supreme Court.

On 30 April 2003, the first charges related to the Bali bombings were made against Amrozi bin Haji Nurhasyim, known as Amrozi, for allegedly buying the explosives and the van used in the bombings. On 8 August, he was found guilty and sentenced to death. Another participant in the bombing, Imam Samudra, was sentenced to death on 10 September. Amrozi's brother, Ali Imron, who had expressed remorse for his part in the bombing, was sentenced to life imprisonment on 18 September. A fourth accused, Ali Ghufron, the brother-in-law of Noordin Mohammed Top was sentenced to death on 1 October. Ali Ghufron, alias Mukhlas, told police that he was the head of one of Jemaah Islamiyah's four cells and had ordered the Bali bombings. He also confessed that a fellow leader Riduan Isamuddin, known as Hambali, had provided the funds for the attacks. He told police,

I do not know for sure the source of the aforementioned money from Hambali; most probably it was from Afghanistan, that is, from Sheikh Usama bin Laden. As far as I know, Hambali did not have a source of funds except from Afghanistan.

Another operative, Wan Min bin Wan Mat, revealed to police that he had given Mukhlas money, at Hambali's request and that he understood part of the money had come directly from al-Qaeda.

EXECUTION OF PERPETRATORS

On 24 October 2008, Bali officials announced that three men convicted of carrying out the bombings would be executed by firing squad in November 2008. On 25 October 2008, Communications and Information Minister asked the Indonesian media to stop calling the three "heroes".

The Denpasar District Court, on 3 November, accepted a reprieve motion to reconsider the death sentences. Fahmi Bachmid, a lawyer for the family of Jafar Sodiq, a brother of Amrozi and Mukhlas, stated: "We lodged the judicial review to Denpasar court to question (previous) decisions." Lawyer Imam Asmara Hadi stated: "We have lodged an appeal because we haven't received a copy of the Supreme Court rejection of our previous appeal."

Indonesia's Supreme Court denied previous petitions for judicial review amid the constitutional court's dismissal of the bombers' appeals. Denpasar court official Nengah Sanjaya said the 3-page appeal would be sent to a Cilacap, central Java court. But the Attorney General's office said on 1 November the execution was "very close". Supreme Court judge Djoko Sarwoko, however, said a "last-minute legal challenge by the relatives of Imam Samudra, Amrozi Nurhasyim and Ali Ghufron will not change or delay the execution." They were moved to isolation cells, and execution spots were ready on the Nusakambangan island prison where they were being held. Local chief prosecutor Muhammad Yamin said they would be "executed simultaneously" but at different locations.

Amrozi, Imam Samudra and Ali Ghufron were executed by firing squad after midnight on 9 November 2008 (West Indonesian time). In the final moment, there was no remorse or repentance, and they shouted: Allahu Akbar, or "God is great!" Despite his carefree demeanor throughout his trial and incarceration, the Australian edition of *The Daily Telegraph* reported Amrozi was pale-faced and shaking in the moments before his execution. For burial, Mukhlas and Amrozi's bodies were flown by helicopter to Tenggulun, Lamongan, East Java, while Imam Samudra's body was flown to Serang, Banten, amid "welcome martyrs" banner displayed at the cemetery.

CONCLUSION

The 2002 Bali bombings were a pivotal moment in the history of terrorism in Southeast Asia. The attack, which claimed the lives of over 200 people and injured hundreds more, shocked the world and marked a significant escalation in the threat posed by Islamist extremism in the region. The bombings not only devastated Bali and Indonesia but also highlighted the global nature of the fight against terrorism.

In the years since the attack, Indonesia and other countries in Southeast Asia have made significant strides in counterterrorism efforts, but the legacy of the Bali bombings continues to resonate in the region and beyond. The attack remains a stark reminder of the threat posed by global terrorism and the need for international cooperation in the fight against extremism. As Southeast Asia continues to grapple with these challenges, the memory of those who lost their lives in the Bali bombings serves as a powerful call to action.

CHAPTER 11
ASHLEY MADISON WEBSITE HACK

SEX SITE FLOORED BY HACKERS

The Ashley Madison website hack, which came to light in the summer of 2015, remains one of the most infamous and impactful cyberattacks in modern internet history. Ashley Madison, a website designed for facilitating extramarital affairs, became the target of a massive data breach that exposed the personal information of millions of its users. The hack not only led to public embarrassment, legal consequences, and a significant loss of trust in the website but also raised important questions about online security, privacy, and ethical behavior in the digital age. This chapter provides a detailed account of the Ashley Madison hack, examining the events surrounding the attack, the consequences for individuals and organizations involved, and the wider implications of the breach for internet security, corporate accountability, and personal privacy.

BACKGROUND OF ASHLEY MADISON

Ashley Madison was launched in 2001 by a company called Avid Life Media, with the slogan "Life is short. Have an affair." The website's primary objective was to provide a platform for people seeking extramarital relationships.

While Ashley Madison's mission was controversial, it gained significant popularity among people looking for discreet encounters outside of their marriages or committed relationships.

At its peak, the site had more than 39 million users from across the globe. It allowed users to create profiles, browse others' profiles, and send messages to potential matches. The site's business model centered around the concept of premium membership, where users could pay for additional services, such as sending messages to other users, browsing through profiles of paid members, or using features like the "Traveling Man" function, which enabled users to see other members in the cities they were visiting.

Ashley Madison's controversial nature made it a target of both praise and criticism. On the one hand, it provided a platform for people to explore relationships outside of traditional norms. On the other hand, it attracted heavy criticism for its role in encouraging infidelity, which led to social stigma and moral outrage from religious and conservative communities. Despite these challenges, the company found success and expanded globally.

THE HACK: INITIAL DISCOVERY

In July 2015, a group of hackers called **The Impact Team** breached the Ashley Madison website. The group's main demand was clear: they wanted the company to shut down its operation. If their demands were not met, the hackers promised to release sensitive data that could potentially ruin the lives of millions of Ashley Madison users. The hack had been planned with precision, and The Impact Team demonstrated their capability by encrypting their message and posting it publicly on the website's server.

The hackers' initial message was both direct and threatening:

"Ashley Madison has been compromised. Your data is now in the wild. We have released all customer information, including all records of cheating. You know the deal... You can delete your profile, but we still have all your data."

On July 19, 2015, The Impact Team made good on their threat, releasing a portion of the stolen data, including email addresses, names, and other personally identifiable information of millions of Ashley Madison users. At this point, the hack escalated from a threat to a public crisis for the company.

DETAILS OF THE HACK: THE DATA LEAK

The Ashley Madison hack was not just a theft of personal information; it was a calculated breach designed to humiliate the website's users. The data leaked by the hackers included sensitive information such as:

- **Names**: Real names of users, many of whom were public figures or professionals with reputations to protect.
- **Email addresses**: Some of the email addresses were linked to other personal or professional accounts.
- **Credit card information**: Payment data, which could potentially reveal the identity of users who paid for subscriptions or made in-app purchases.
- **Messages and chat logs**: Communications between users that demonstrated their engagement in extramarital or illicit affairs.
- **Geolocation data**: Locations where users accessed the site, potentially linking individuals to specific geographic regions or activities.

The data dump quickly gained the attention of media outlets, and the hacked information began circulating online. The hackers also leaked over 9.7 gigabytes of data, which included:

- **User profiles**: Names, dates of birth, addresses, and other personally identifiable information.
- **Chat and transactional history**: Conversations between users, some of which were explicit, and details of payments made for premium services.
- **Administrative data**: Information about the website's internal systems, which could reveal vulnerabilities and provide further insight into how Ashley Madison operated.

The hackers even released user emails in batches, making it clear that the information was in the hands of the public. In some cases, prominent figures, including politicians, business executives, and military personnel, were among those whose private data was exposed. The leak immediately became a global scandal, as individuals and families began to experience the fallout from the hack.

IMPACT ON INDIVIDUALS: PUBLIC SHAMING AND PERSONAL CONSEQUENCES

The Ashley Madison hack had significant personal consequences for millions of people. The leak of sensitive data exposed many users' extramarital affairs, leading to public embarrassment and personal anguish. Many individuals who had sought anonymity found themselves in the spotlight, their private lives and actions laid bare for anyone to see.

For some, the consequences were even more severe. Multiple reports indicated that individuals who had been exposed by the leak suffered from mental health crises, including depression, anxiety, and suicidal thoughts. A number of individuals lost their jobs, as their involvement in infidelity conflicted with their professional roles or ethical standards. In certain cases, relationships and marriages were irreparably damaged. Some individuals lost their livelihoods or faced public shaming in their communities.

The hack also led to a significant spike in divorce filings. Attorneys reported that the exposure of Ashley Madison users' information contributed to a rise in divorce cases, with many spouses seeking legal action against their unfaithful partners.

Perhaps one of the most tragic consequences of the breach was the alleged suicides of individuals who were affected by the leak. Several individuals, including at least two men, were reported to have taken their own lives after their personal information was revealed. The tragedy underscored the potential dangers of such a public data breach, particularly for people whose lives were already in delicate situations.

THE LEGAL FALLOUT: LAWSUITS AND INVESTIGATIONS

The Ashley Madison hack also triggered a series of legal actions. In the wake of the breach, the company was sued by multiple parties, including individuals whose personal data had been exposed. Several lawsuits claimed that Avid Life Media, the parent company of Ashley Madison, had been negligent in safeguarding user information and protecting its platform from attacks.

One of the most prominent class-action lawsuits was filed in Canada, where Avid Life Media is headquartered. The lawsuit accused the company of failing to adequately protect users' data and of misleading individuals about the level of security on the site. The plaintiffs argued that the company was responsible for the privacy violations and the psychological distress that resulted from the leak.

In the United States, other lawsuits were filed by both individual users and organizations affected by the breach. The lawsuits often focused on claims of negligence, invasion of privacy, and violations of data protection laws. Many users sought compensation for the emotional and financial damage caused by the leak.

In addition to the legal ramifications for the company, investigations were launched to determine the perpetrators of the hack. Law enforcement agencies, including the FBI and Canadian authorities, began looking into the identities of the hackers. The investigation led to questions about the motivations behind the attack, with some speculating that the hackers were driven by ideological beliefs against infidelity, while others believed the attack was financially motivated, as the hackers demanded the website's closure in exchange for the return of stolen data.

CORPORATE ACCOUNTABILITY AND THE RESPONSE FROM AVID LIFE MEDIA

In the aftermath of the Ashley Madison hack, Avid Life Media (the company behind the website) faced intense scrutiny for its handling of the breach. Many critics argued that the company had been too focused on profit generation to ensure the security of its users' sensitive information. At the time of the hack, the site had been storing massive amounts of personal data about its users without employing sufficient cybersecurity measures. For example, it was revealed that Ashley Madison used weak encryption practices to protect user data, leaving it vulnerable to attack.

In response to the breach, Avid Life Media's CEO, Noel Biderman, initially downplayed the severity of the attack and promised that the company would take steps to secure its platform in the future. However, the damage was already done. The company's reputation was irreparably harmed, and it became embroiled in a public relations disaster.

In addition to the damage to its brand, Avid Life Media faced financial repercussions as well. The company spent millions of dollars on legal fees, security upgrades, and public relations efforts. The company's finances were also impacted by the significant drop in user subscriptions and the mass cancellation of accounts after the breach.

Biderman himself eventually resigned as CEO in the wake of the scandal, and the company went through several rounds of restructuring and leadership changes. Despite these efforts to rebuild, Avid Life Media never fully recovered from the scandal.

ETHICAL AND PHILOSOPHICAL IMPLICATIONS: PRIVACY VS. PUBLIC SHAMING

The Ashley Madison hack raised several ethical and philosophical questions about privacy, data security, and public shaming. At the heart of the issue was the question of whether it was justifiable to expose the private lives of millions of individuals for the sake of punishing an organization or promoting moral ideals.

On one hand, the hack exposed the hypocrisy and deceit of an organization that profited from infidelity, and many felt that Ashley Madison had taken advantage of vulnerable individuals seeking anonymity in their personal lives. Some viewed the hackers as vigilantes, targeting a website that many considered morally objectionable. There were calls from certain quarters to hold such platforms accountable for enabling extramarital affairs and contributing to societal harm.

On the other hand, the hack raised serious concerns about the dangers of public shaming and the potential consequences of exposing people's private information. Critics argued that the hackers were engaging in a form of vigilante justice that violated individuals' privacy rights and harmed people who had not consented to having their personal lives exposed. The widespread release of sensitive information triggered debates about the ethical responsibilities of hackers and the right to privacy in the digital age.

IMPACT ON CYBERSECURITY AND FUTURE LESSONS

The Ashley Madison hack highlighted the vulnerabilities of online platforms, especially those that store sensitive personal information. The breach raised awareness of the need for stronger cybersecurity measures, particularly for websites that handle user data, including financial information, personal messages, and communications.

The attack underscored the importance of encryption and secure data storage. Ashley Madison's weak encryption practices were cited as one of the key reasons why the hack was successful. Following the incident, many companies in the online dating and other high-risk sectors reevaluated their security measures, implementing stricter protocols to protect user data from cyberattacks.

The hack also prompted regulatory changes in the tech and cybersecurity industries. In the years following the Ashley Madison breach, there were renewed efforts to enforce data protection laws, such as the **General Data Protection Regulation (GDPR)** in Europe, which mandates stricter protections for personal data.

CHAPTER 12
THE DARFUR GENOCIDE
A CHAPTER IN HUMANITY'S DARKEST HISTORY

The Darfur Genocide, a catastrophic event that took place from 2003 onwards in Sudan's western region of Darfur, stands as a stark reminder of the horrors humanity is capable of. This chapter seeks to explore the political, social, and historical dynamics that led to the Darfur Genocide, the violent atrocities that occurred, and the lasting impact of these events on the people of Sudan and the global community.

Omar Hassan Ahmad al-Bashir

THE ROAD TO DARFUR: POLITICAL AND HISTORICAL BACKGROUND

Darfur, a region located in the western part of Sudan, had long been a historically marginalized area in the context of Sudanese politics. Sudan, Africa's largest country geographically, has been plagued by centuries of ethnic and political conflict. The ethnic composition of the country is diverse, with a complex interplay of Arab and African groups, each with its own distinct culture, language, and history. The Arab groups, largely located in the north, have historically held power, while the African groups, spread out across the country, particularly in the south and the west, have often found themselves relegated to positions of political and economic subordination.

Darfur, while distinct from the long-running conflict between the Arab-dominated Sudanese government and the African populations in the south, was nonetheless subjected to similar patterns of neglect. The region, sparsely populated and primarily rural, had historically been one of the poorest areas of Sudan. It lacked access to basic infrastructure, education, and healthcare. As with many parts of Africa, the colonial legacy also played a significant role in shaping Sudan's political landscape. The British colonial rulers administered Sudan as two separate regions, the Arab North and the African South, without fostering any real unity between the two. This sowed the seeds for future division.

Following Sudan's independence from Britain in 1956, tensions between the northern Arab elites and the southern African populations escalated into a series of civil wars. In 1983, the second Sudanese civil war broke out, primarily between the northern government, which was dominated by Arab Muslims, and the southern rebels, who were mostly African and Christian or animist. The war lasted until 2005, claiming over two million lives and leaving millions more displaced. The 2005 peace agreement that ended the war gave hope for peace and stability in Sudan, but the country's political structure remained fragile.

Darfur, however, was not immune to the political instability and inequality that plagued Sudan. The region, which is home to various ethnic groups including the Fur, Zaghawa, and Masalit, had long experienced tensions with the central government in Khartoum. These tensions were exacerbated by the fact that Darfur had long been neglected by the Sudanese government in terms of economic development and political representation. While the government in Khartoum focused its resources and attention on the more prosperous northern regions, Darfur remained mired in poverty.

The crisis in Darfur, however, did not fully emerge until the early 2000s. In 2003, a coalition of rebel groups in Darfur the Sudan Liberation Movement/Army (SLM/A) and the Justice and Equality Movement (JEM) began to wage an armed revolt against the government. Their main grievances were the same as those of other marginalized groups: political exclusion, economic inequality, and the government's failure to address the needs of the region. These rebel groups accused the Sudanese government of using force to suppress dissent and oppress the region's African population.

The Sudanese government's response to the rebellion was swift and brutal. Khartoum, under the leadership of President Omar al-Bashir, accused the rebel groups of being agents of foreign powers and sought to put down the rebellion through military force. In doing so, the government unleashed a campaign of mass violence that would become the Darfur Genocide.

THE UNLEASHING OF VIOLENCE: THE ROLE OF JANJAWEED MILITIAS

In response to the Darfur insurgency, the Sudanese government began to arm and support a group of militia forces made up primarily of Arab fighters known as the Janjaweed. The Janjaweed, meaning "devils on horseback," became infamous for their role in carrying out atrocities against the African civilians of Darfur. The militias, which were loosely organized and often acted independently, were given free rein to attack African villages suspected of supporting the rebel groups.

The Janjaweed were responsible for a wide range of violent acts, including the systematic burning of villages, mass killings, rapes, and other forms of sexual violence, as well as widespread torture and abuse. They targeted civilians indiscriminately, regardless of age or gender, and sought to instill fear and terror in the population. It was a campaign of ethnic cleansing, with African villagers being deliberately displaced from their homes and communities.

The government, while publicly denying its involvement in the atrocities, provided logistical and material support to the Janjaweed militias. This included supplying them with weapons, vehicles, and other resources, as well as offering air support through bombings and aerial attacks. The government's role in the violence was clear, even though it denied any direct connection to the militias' actions.

The Janjaweed's campaign of violence was not confined to specific rebel-controlled areas but spread across the region, targeting both the rural populations and the urban centers. Towns and villages were attacked, and the people living there were subjected to forced displacement. Whole communities were uprooted, and the survivors were left to wander in the desert, vulnerable to further violence and death.

The Sudanese government's tactics were also aimed at preventing any form of resistance from the African population. Villages were burned to the ground, and crops were destroyed, ensuring that the people would have no means of survival. As a result, many of the displaced were forced into overcrowded and unsanitary refugee camps, where they faced further threats of violence, disease, and starvation.

INTERNATIONAL RESPONSE: THE FAILURE OF THE GLOBAL COMMUNITY

As the violence escalated in Darfur, the international community began to take notice. However, the response was slow and often inadequate. Early reports from the United Nations and various humanitarian organizations indicated that the situation in Darfur was dire, with widespread atrocities being committed against civilians. However, it wasn't until 2004 that the international community began to acknowledge the full extent of the violence and its genocidal nature.

The United States, in particular, played a prominent role in labeling the events in Darfur as genocide. In 2004, U.S. Secretary of State Colin Powell declared that the Sudanese government's actions in Darfur constituted "genocide," making the U.S. one of the first countries to make an official statement on the matter. The United Nations, however, was more hesitant. The UN's response was hindered by political considerations and a lack of consensus among its members. Russia and China, both of whom had close relations with the Sudanese government, blocked stronger measures from being taken.

In the face of such inaction, humanitarian organizations took it upon themselves to provide aid and raise awareness about the crisis. Groups like Doctors Without Borders and the International Committee of the Red Cross were instrumental in providing medical care and basic necessities to the displaced populations. However, their efforts were often thwarted by the ongoing violence and the Sudanese government's obstruction of aid efforts.

The United Nations eventually authorized the deployment of peacekeeping forces to Darfur under the banner of the African Union-United Nations Hybrid Operation in Darfur (UNAMID) in 2007. However, these peacekeepers were hampered by limited resources, lack of support from the Sudanese government, and the ongoing dangers posed by the Janjaweed militias. The peacekeeping mission, while attempting to stabilize the region, was largely ineffective in preventing further atrocities.

THE AFTERMATH: THE TOLL OF THE DARFUR GENOCIDE

The toll of the Darfur Genocide is staggering. Estimates of the death toll vary, but it is widely believed that between 200,000 and 400,000 people were killed during the course of the violence, while millions were displaced from their homes. Hundreds of thousands of women and girls were subjected to rape and sexual violence, and the psychological scars of the violence will persist for generations.

The impact of the genocide extended far beyond the immediate violence. The destruction of villages, homes, and livelihoods left the population of Darfur in a state of despair. Refugee camps became the new home for many, where access to food, clean water, and healthcare remained limited. The social fabric of Darfur was shattered, and the hope for a return to normalcy seemed increasingly distant.

The Sudanese government's refusal to cooperate with international authorities, including the International Criminal Court (ICC), further compounded the situation. In 2009, the ICC issued an arrest warrant for President Omar al-Bashir, charging him with war crimes, crimes against humanity, and genocide. Despite the warrant, al-Bashir remained in power until his ousting in 2019, and the atrocities continued unabated during his rule.

LEGACY AND THE ONGOING STRUGGLE FOR JUSTICE

The Darfur Genocide has left an indelible mark on the people of Sudan and the global community. While the international community's response was widely criticized as too slow and ineffective, the genocide sparked greater awareness of the need for international intervention in cases of mass atrocities.

However, despite efforts to bring those responsible for the violence to justice, the situation in Darfur remains unresolved. While al-Bashir was eventually arrested and tried, many of the perpetrators of the violence in Darfur have yet to be held accountable. The region continues to experience instability, with rebel groups still fighting for autonomy and justice.

The legacy of the Darfur Genocide serves as a somber reminder of the capacity for cruelty and indifference in the face of human suffering. The world cannot afford to forget the atrocities committed in Darfur, and the fight for justice and accountability must continue. The survivors of the genocide and the people of Darfur deserve justice, and it is up to the global community to ensure that such horrors are never repeated.

AL BASHIR DETENTION & TRIALS

On 17 April 2019, al-Bashir was moved from house arrest to Khartoum's Kobar Prison. On 13 May 2019, prosecutors charged al-Bashir with "inciting and participating in" the killing of protesters. A trial for corruption (after $130 million was found in his home and money laundering against al-Bashir started during the following months. On 14 December 2019, he was convicted for money laundering and corruption. He was sentenced to two years in prison.

On 21 July 2020, his trial regarding the coup that brought him to power started. About 20 military personnel were indicted for their roles in the coup. On 20 December 2022, al-Bashir said that he bears full responsibility for the events that took place in the country on June 30, 1989. The trial was expected to continue for several more months and if convicted, Bashir could face a death sentence.

INTERNATIONAL CRIMINAL COURT

On 5 November 2019, the Forces of Freedom and Change alliance (FFC), which holds indirect political power during the 39 month Sudanese transition to democracy stated that it had reached a consensus decision in favor of transferring al-Bashir to the ICC after the completion of his corruption and money laundering trial in the following days, Sudanese transition period Prime Minister Abdalla Hamdok and Sovereignty Council member Siddiq Tawer stated that al-Bashir would be transferred to the JCC. On 11 February 2020, Sudan's ruling military council agreed to hand over the ousted al-Bashir to the ICC in The Hague to face charges of crimes against humanity in Darfur. In October 2020, ICC Chief Prosecutor Fatou Bensouda and a delegation arrived in Sudan to discuss with the government about Bashir's indictment. In a deal with Darfurian rebels, the government agreed to set up a special war crimes court that would include Bashir.

DETENTION[

On 26 April 2023, the Sudanese Armed Forces stated that al-Bashir, Bakri Hassan Saleh, Abdel Rahim Mohammed Hussein and two other former officials were taken from Kobar Prison to Alia Military Hospital in Omdurman due to the conflict that erupted earlier that month. Al-Bashir and other officials were later taken to a hospital at Wadi Seidna Air Base, where they remained until their transfer to a facility in Merowe in September 2024. Al Bashir awaits justice whilst suffering ill health due to a heart condition.

CHAPTER 13
MARTHA STEWART INSIDER TRADING SCANDAL
THE SPECTACULAR DOWNFALL OF A TV SUPERSTAR

Martha Stewart, a household name synonymous with domestic perfection, cooking, and lifestyle expertise, once found herself at the center of a high-profile scandal that shook the business world. The Martha Stewart insider trading case is one of the most notorious instances of corporate misdeeds and celebrity entanglement in modern American history. A case that transcended the typical bounds of Wall Street scandal, involving a celebrity mogul whose personal brand and immense public influence added layers of intrigue and complexity worldwide.

THE RISE OF MARTHA STEWART: A HOUSEHOLD NAME

Before the scandal, Martha Stewart was an emblem of American success, widely regarded as a pioneer in the realm of home decorating, cooking, and entertaining. Stewart built a vast empire from her early days as a stockbroker to her later ventures into publishing, television, and product licensing. Her television show, *Martha Stewart Living*, was an institution, and her books on cooking, gardening, and homemaking were bestsellers. She became a symbol of grace, wealth, and sophistication.

Stewart's company, Martha Stewart Living Omnimedia (MSO), was a powerful entity in the media and lifestyle industries. She presided over a multimedia brand that included a magazine, television network, product lines, and a burgeoning online presence. In the early 2000s, Stewart's brand was synonymous with affluence and style, and she was, in many ways, the queen of American homemaking.

But in 2001, Stewart's glittering empire began to crack under the weight of a criminal investigation. It was not her business practices, her television productions, or her brand that brought her down. It was an event in the stock market—a moment of temptation that would alter the course of her career and legacy.

UNDERSTANDING INSIDER TRADING

Insider trading is a term that often pops up in news headlines, particularly when there is talk about illegal activities in the stock market. It refers to the buying or selling of a company's stocks, bonds, or other securities by individuals who have access to non-public, material information about the company. This information is considered "insider" knowledge and is not available to the general public, which gives those with access an unfair advantage in the marketplace.

The core idea behind insider trading is that some people, usually executives, employees, or other insiders of a company, have access to important information that could influence the stock price. If these individuals act on that knowledge—by buying or selling stocks before the information is made public—they are engaging in insider trading. This is illegal because it undermines the fairness of the financial markets, where everyone should have access to the same information when making investment decisions.

To better understand insider trading, it is essential to break down the concept into a few key points:

WHAT MAKES INFORMATION "MATERIAL"?

In the context of insider trading, the word "material" refers to information that could influence an investor's decision to buy or sell a stock. This could be anything that has the potential to impact the financial performance or outlook of a company. For example, if a company is about to announce a groundbreaking new product or is involved in a merger, this could significantly affect its stock price. Information like that, which is not yet public, is considered material.

THE ROLE OF INSIDER INFORMATION

Insider information can come from various sources within the company. Top executives like CEOs, CFOs, or other employees who are privy to sensitive data might use that knowledge to trade stocks before the information becomes widely known. For instance, if a company's earnings report is better than expected, an executive might buy shares before the report is publicly released to profit from the anticipated rise in stock price once the news breaks.

LEGAL VS. ILLEGAL INSIDER TRADING

It's important to note that not all insider trading is illegal. In fact, there are instances where insiders can legally buy and sell their company's stock. For example, insiders can make trades as long as they follow certain rules, such as making the transactions through a pre-established plan (often referred to as a "10b5-1 plan"), which is a legal way to avoid accusations of insider trading. These plans are set up at a time when the individual is not aware of any material non-public information.

CONSEQUENCES OF ILLEGAL INSIDER TRADING

When individuals engage in illegal insider trading, the penalties can be severe. The U.S. Securities and Exchange Commission (SEC) is responsible for investigating and prosecuting cases of insider trading. If someone is found guilty, they can face hefty fines, jail time, or both. In some high-profile cases, individuals have faced millions of dollars in fines, as well as lengthy prison sentences.

WHY INSIDER TRADING IS HARMFUL

Insider trading is harmful to the fairness and integrity of the stock market. It creates an uneven playing field where those with privileged information can profit at the expense of ordinary investors who do not have access to that same information. This erodes trust in the financial markets, which can discourage people from investing, ultimately harming the economy.

Insider trading, whether legal or illegal, plays a significant role in how the stock market functions. While legal insider trading is permissible under certain conditions, illegal insider trading is a serious offense with significant consequences. It undermines the fairness of the financial markets, and it is crucial for investors and insiders alike to understand the rules to maintain a level playing field.

THE INSIDER TRADING ALLEGATION: THE STOCK SALE OF IMCLONE SYSTEMS

The origins of the scandal can be traced back to one fateful day in December 2001. Stewart owned a substantial amount of stock in a biotechnology company called ImClone Systems, a company specializing in cancer treatment drugs. At the time, ImClone's stock was under pressure after the U.S. Food and Drug Administration (FDA) rejected a key cancer drug developed by the company, Erbitux. The rejection caused the company's stock to plummet, and investors began to panic.

It was at this moment that Martha Stewart sold 4,000 shares of her ImClone stock. What made this transaction particularly suspicious was that Stewart sold her shares just one day before the FDA announcement about the rejection. Stewart's decision to sell her stock raised eyebrows, but it wasn't the sale alone that led to the investigation. It was the timing and the circumstances surrounding her knowledge of the upcoming news.

Stewart's actions caught the attention of regulators, including the U.S. Securities and Exchange Commission (SEC). Questions began to swirl: how did Stewart know to sell her shares before the news of the FDA rejection became public? Was there a possibility that she had received non-public, confidential information from someone with insider knowledge of the FDA decision?

The tipping point came when it was revealed that Stewart had been informed of the impending FDA decision by her broker, Peter Bacanovic, who worked at the brokerage firm Merrill Lynch. Bacanovic was a former stockbroker who had been involved with Stewart's financial affairs for several years. According to investigators, Bacanovic had tipped Stewart off about the FDA's rejection of ImClone's drug, which caused her to sell her shares in advance of the news.

THE INVESTIGATION AND LEGAL RAMIFICATIONS

Following the suspicious sale, the SEC and the U.S. Attorney's Office launched a thorough investigation into Stewart's trading activity. The investigation soon focused on whether she had engaged in insider trading, which involves buying or selling stocks based on non-public, material information that could affect the stock's value.

In 2002, Bacanovic and Stewart were both charged with obstruction of justice, conspiracy, and securities fraud. The government alleged that Stewart and Bacanovic had conspired to avoid losses by illegally trading on the basis of confidential information. Bacanovic was accused of telling Stewart about the FDA's rejection before it was publicly known, allowing her to sell her shares at a much higher price than she would have been able to after the news broke.

Both Bacanovic and Stewart denied the allegations. Stewart maintained that her decision to sell her shares was based on a pre-arranged stop-loss order, meaning that the sale had been made based on a previous agreement to sell the stock if it fell to a certain price. Stewart claimed that she had no knowledge of the FDA decision before selling her stock and that her actions were entirely legal.

Despite these denials, the case quickly became a media sensation. Stewart, once a beloved media figure, was now being scrutinized in a public spectacle that captivated the nation. The legal battle would ultimately become a test of the judicial system's ability to hold powerful figures accountable and of the public's willingness to hold celebrities to the same legal standards as ordinary citizens.

THE TRIAL AND CONVICTION: THE CONSEQUENCES OF CELEBRITY AND WEALTH

In 2004, the case went to trial in the Southern District of New York. The government argued that Stewart and Bacanovic had engaged in a conspiracy to cover up their actions, presenting evidence that the timing of the stock sale and the information Stewart had received about ImClone's drug approval had been crucial. The prosecution also emphasized that Stewart had lied to investigators, obstructed the SEC's inquiry, and misled the public about the reasons for her stock sale.

Stewart's defense team countered these allegations by presenting evidence that Stewart had acted on the advice of Bacanovic, who had allegedly assured her that the stock sale was in line with her financial interests. The defense also suggested that there was no conclusive evidence that Stewart had known about the FDA's rejection before selling her shares.

Despite the absence of direct evidence linking Stewart to insider trading, the jury ultimately found her guilty of obstruction of justice and making false statements. She was acquitted of the securities fraud charge, which would have required a direct link between her stock sale and the non-public information she allegedly received. Nonetheless, the conviction was significant, as it sent a powerful message about the consequences of using one's position for personal gain, regardless of celebrity status.

In 2004, Stewart was sentenced to five months in prison, five months of home confinement, and two years of probation. She was also fined $30,000. Bacanovic was sentenced to serve a prison term of five years, although he was later released after serving a reduced sentence. The sentences shocked the public, as many believed that Stewart's celebrity status should have afforded her a different treatment. Still, the conviction set a precedent for accountability in cases of white-collar crime, particularly those involving high-profile figures.

THE IMPACT ON STEWART'S BRAND AND CAREER

Martha Stewart's conviction had a dramatic effect on her career. For a woman who had spent decades building her empire, the legal fallout was catastrophic. Her stock in Martha Stewart Living Omnimedia plummeted, as investors feared the long-term impact of her legal troubles on the brand. Several of Stewart's corporate partners, including Kmart, severed their business ties with her in the wake of the scandal.

Stewart's popular television show, *Martha Stewart Living*, was canceled, and she was publicly vilified by many for her involvement in the scandal. The negative press coverage and legal proceedings left Stewart with little opportunity to maintain her public persona as the nation's homemaking queen.

Yet, Stewart was resilient. Rather than retreat into obscurity, she made a remarkable comeback. Stewart served her prison sentence, and following her release, she began to rebuild her brand. She returned to television with a new show, *The Martha Stewart Show*, which found success and helped restore her public image. Her business ventures continued, and over the next decade, Stewart was able to re-establish her presence in the media and lifestyle industries.

Her ability to bounce back from the scandal and rebuild her empire demonstrated the tenacity and resourcefulness that had originally made her a household name. However, the scandal would forever be a part of her legacy, reminding the public that even the most polished and successful figures could fall from grace.

BROADER IMPLICATIONS AND LESSONS LEARNED

The Martha Stewart insider trading scandal had far-reaching implications for both corporate America and celebrity culture. On the one hand, it demonstrated that even the most powerful and famous figures could be held accountable for breaking the law. The case was a reminder that no one, regardless of wealth or fame, was above the law.

It also highlighted the risks associated with insider trading, a crime that remains one of the most serious violations in the financial world. The scandal reinforced the importance of transparency in the stock market and the need for strong regulatory oversight to prevent abuses of power.

For celebrities, the case served as a cautionary tale about the consequences of intertwining personal interests with business dealings. Stewart's case showed that the public's perception of a celebrity can shift dramatically when the person is involved in a legal scandal. Her fall from grace was swift, and it underscored the fragility of fame in the face of serious allegations.

CONCLUSION: A LEGACY REWRITTEN

The Martha Stewart insider trading scandal remains one of the most memorable white-collar crime cases in American history. It exposed the darker side of celebrity, corporate America, and the world of stock trading. Yet, in the aftermath, Stewart's ability to recover and rebuild her brand served as a testament to her resilience and business acumen.

Today, Martha Stewart is no longer just a symbol of perfection in the home but a figure who has overcome personal and professional challenges to reinvent herself. The scandal may have tarnished her reputation, but it also cemented her legacy as a woman who faced adversity head-on and emerged stronger.

The Martha Stewart insider trading scandal serves as both a cautionary tale and a story of redemption—one that continues to captivate and intrigue the public.

CHAPTER 14
THE #ME TOO MOVEMENT
OUTING THE PREDATORS

The #MeToo movement, which ignited a global conversation about sexual harassment and assault, is one of the most significant social movements of the 21st century. It gave a voice to countless individuals who had suffered in silence, provided a platform for survivors to share their stories, and helped bring about tangible changes in policies, workplace norms, and social attitudes toward sexual misconduct.

#Me Too Protest

TARANA BURKE AND THE FOUNDING OF THE "ME TOO" MOVEMENT

The #MeToo movement, as it is widely recognized today, has its roots in the work of Tarana Burke, an activist and social justice advocate. Long before the viral hashtag spread across social media platforms in 2017, Burke was working tirelessly to raise awareness about the sexual violence and abuse faced by women, particularly women of color.

In 2006, Tarana Burke coined the phrase "Me Too" as a part of her work with young women in marginalized communities. Burke, who was living in New York City at the time, was working with young girls who had experienced sexual abuse. She saw firsthand how they struggled with the shame and silence surrounding their experiences. Burke wanted to create a safe space where survivors could talk about their experiences without fear of judgment or reprisal.

Burke's work was particularly focused on young women of color, many of whom had no resources or platforms to share their stories. Her goal was not just to provide emotional support but to help women and girls reclaim their voices and take control of their narratives. She began using the phrase "Me Too" to show solidarity with these young survivors, to let them know that they were not alone. The phrase was meant to be empowering and validating — to tell women, particularly women from marginalized communities, that their experiences mattered.

Despite her early efforts, the movement remained relatively small and under the radar. Burke, who had faced significant personal and professional challenges as a result of her activism, continued her work quietly, focusing on organizing grassroots initiatives and helping those in need. However, the lack of widespread attention did not diminish the importance of the message she was spreading: sexual violence and harassment are pervasive, and survivors deserve support and recognition.

EARLY CONVERSATIONS ABOUT SEXUAL HARASSMENT

Before the advent of the #MeToo hashtag, conversations about sexual harassment and assault were often confined to private discussions or small-scale activist groups. High-profile cases of sexual misconduct, such as the 1991 hearings for Clarence Thomas, the U.S. Supreme Court nominee accused of sexual harassment by Anita Hill, and the public discussions about the sexual abuse allegations surrounding figures like Bill Cosby, brought attention to these issues, but the mainstream conversation was still limited.

In the decades before the #MeToo movement gained prominence, there was a growing awareness of workplace sexual harassment, particularly following the landmark 1986 Supreme Court ruling in *Meritor Savings Bank v. Vinson*. This case helped define sexual harassment as a form of discrimination under Title VII of the Civil Rights Act of 1964, laying the groundwork for future legal action and activism around the issue.

While such legal milestones and individual stories had made headway in shaping public understanding of sexual harassment, the issue still lacked the widespread recognition that would later emerge. Survivors were often hesitant to come forward, fearing retribution or not being believed, and public discussions on sexual misconduct were still frequently minimized or dismissed as personal matters.

THE CATALYST: HARVEY WEINSTEIN AND THE 2017 NEW YORK TIMES INVESTIGATION

The modern #MeToo movement is often seen as a response to the Harvey Weinstein scandal, which erupted in 2017. Weinstein, once a powerful Hollywood mogul, was accused by multiple women of sexual harassment, assault, and rape. The initial reporting by *The New York Times* on October 5, 2017, revealed a pattern of systematic abuse that spanned decades, and the allegations against Weinstein sparked a domino effect, with other women coming forward to accuse him of similar misconduct.

Weinstein's actions were not an isolated incident but rather part of a broader culture of sexual harassment that permeated the entertainment industry, as well as many other sectors. The scale and scope of the allegations against Weinstein demonstrated how entrenched and pervasive sexual abuse could be within powerful institutions.

The significance of the New York Times investigation cannot be overstated. It served as a turning point in the way society viewed sexual harassment and abuse. For years, women had tried to come forward with their stories of Weinstein's abuse, but they were met with silence, intimidation, or disbelief. The power of Weinstein's position in Hollywood made it difficult for many women to speak out.

However, the investigative reporting by journalists Jodi Kantor and Megan Twohey allowed these stories to be heard on a national platform. This coverage exposed the systemic nature of Weinstein's abuses and the complicity of Hollywood's culture in enabling such behavior. It was a watershed moment, but it was also just the beginning of a much larger reckoning.

#METOO GOES VIRAL: ALYSSA MILANO AND THE HASHTAG

The spark for the viral spread of #MeToo came shortly after the publication of the New York Times investigation. On October 15, 2017, actress Alyssa Milano, who had herself been a victim of sexual harassment, tweeted a call to action to her followers:

"If you've been sexually harassed or assaulted write 'me too' as a reply to this tweet."

Milano's tweet, which was retweeted by millions, prompted a tidal wave of responses from women (and some men) around the world who used the hashtag #MeToo to share their own experiences of sexual violence. The hashtag provided a space for survivors to share their stories, express solidarity, and raise awareness about the scale of the problem.

In the days following Milano's tweet, #MeToo spread across social media like wildfire, reaching beyond Hollywood to other sectors of society. Women from all walks of life — from political figures and celebrities to everyday women — began to share their stories of harassment and assault. The hashtag became an international movement, shedding light on how widespread sexual violence was and how it transcended borders, industries, and socioeconomic classes.

THE IMPACT OF SOCIAL MEDIA IN AMPLIFYING #METOO

Social media played a critical role in the rapid spread of #MeToo. The viral nature of platforms like Twitter, Facebook, and Instagram allowed the movement to gain traction quickly and reach a global audience. Hashtags, in particular, became an effective way to organize collective action and raise awareness about social issues.

The #MeToo movement harnessed the power of social media to democratize the conversation about sexual harassment. Survivors no longer had to rely solely on mainstream media or legal institutions to have their voices heard. Instead, they could use the hashtag to take control of their own narratives and share their experiences directly with the public. This accessibility made it possible for people who had never had a platform before to participate in the conversation.

As #MeToo spread, it inspired similar movements in other parts of the world, amplifying the voices of survivors who had long been silenced. In countries such as India, the United Kingdom, and South Korea, the hashtag was used to raise awareness of sexual violence and challenge existing cultural norms and practices that perpetuated harassment and assault.

THE WIDE-REACHING IMPACT OF #METOO

The entertainment industry was at the forefront of the #MeToo movement, as many of the first high-profile allegations came from actresses who had worked with Harvey Weinstein. The movement forced the industry to confront its complicity in enabling sexual misconduct, and several powerful figures, including Weinstein, producer Brett Ratner, actor Kevin Spacey, and comedian Louis C.K., were accused of various forms of sexual harassment and abuse.

The fallout from these revelations was swift. Weinstein was fired from his own company, The Weinstein Company, and eventually arrested and charged with sexual assault. Other celebrities faced similar consequences, with several losing their jobs, public roles, or endorsements as a result of the allegations.

Perhaps one of the most striking effects of the #MeToo movement in Hollywood was the sense of solidarity it created among survivors. Actresses like Reese Witherspoon, Shonda Rhimes, and Oprah Winfrey used their platforms to speak out and support other survivors, urging others in the industry to break their silence and join the conversation.

In addition to holding perpetrators accountable, #MeToo led to concrete changes in the industry. In the wake of the movement, Hollywood began to take sexual harassment claims more seriously, with many studios and networks implementing new policies and training programs to prevent sexual misconduct. The movement also brought attention to the gender inequalities and systemic discrimination that had long been prevalent in the entertainment industry.

POLITICAL AND CORPORATE SECTORS

While Hollywood was the initial epicenter of #MeToo, the movement quickly spread to other sectors of society. In the political realm, high-profile allegations were made against U.S. Senator Al Franken, Missouri Governor Eric Greitens, and Alabama Senate candidate Roy Moore, among others. These allegations prompted intense public debate about the role of sexual misconduct in politics and whether individuals who had been accused of such behavior should be held to the same standard as others.

In response to #MeToo, some political institutions took action to address sexual harassment. In the U.S. Senate, for example, new policies were implemented to make it easier for victims of sexual harassment to come forward without facing retaliation. Corporations, too, began to rethink their approach to sexual misconduct in the workplace, introducing new reporting mechanisms, policies, and training programs to prevent harassment and support survivors.

CRITICISMS AND CONTROVERSIES SURROUNDING #METOO

As #MeToo gained momentum, it was not without its critics. Some people argued that the movement unfairly vilified men and created a culture of fear in which men were afraid to interact with women in the workplace or social settings. Others questioned the fairness of "trial by social media" and the potential for false accusations.

Additionally, some critics raised concerns about the way the movement seemed to focus on high-profile cases involving well-known individuals, rather than addressing the broader, everyday occurrences of sexual harassment that many women face in workplaces, schools, and other settings. Others pointed out that the experiences of women of color, trans women, and working-class women were often overlooked in the mainstream #MeToo conversation.

While these criticisms were important to consider, the #MeToo movement ultimately catalyzed a global shift in how sexual harassment and abuse are viewed. It helped create a platform for those whose voices had been ignored or marginalized, and it led to changes in policies, attitudes, and behaviors across various sectors.

CONCLUSION: THE LEGACY OF THE #METOO MOVEMENT

The #MeToo movement has undeniably transformed society's understanding of sexual harassment and abuse. It empowered individuals to speak out, brought attention to pervasive issues that had long been swept under the rug, and forced institutions to confront their complicity in perpetuating sexual violence. While challenges remain, particularly in terms of ensuring justice for all survivors and addressing the deep cultural norms that perpetuate harassment, the #MeToo movement has made a lasting impact on how sexual misconduct is addressed in both the public and private spheres.

By amplifying the voices of survivors and giving them the platform to share their stories, the #MeToo movement has inspired a global reckoning with sexual violence and helped create a new era of accountability. Though the journey is far from over, the movement has opened the door to greater awareness, empathy, and systemic change.

CHAPTER 15
THE TRAFFICKING OF HUMAN ORGANS
SELLING ORGANS FOR HARD CASH

THE RISE OF ORGAN TRAFFICKING: A DETAILED ACCOUNT

Organ trafficking, the illegal trade in human organs, has become one of the most pressing and disturbing global challenges of the 21st century. It involves the illegal buying and selling of human organs, often through coercive or exploitative means, for transplantation purposes. The rise of this illicit market can be attributed to a combination of factors, including the global shortage of organs for transplant, the increasing demand for organ transplants, and the vulnerabilities of both donors and recipients. This 4000-word account seeks to explore the origins, drivers, and consequences of organ trafficking, as well as the efforts made to combat this illegal and harmful trade.

UNDERSTANDING ORGAN TRAFFICKING

Organ trafficking involves the illegal trade of human organs, which are bought and sold on the black market. Typically, traffickers act as intermediaries, connecting people in desperate need of a transplant with those willing to sell their organs, often for a fraction of their true value. The organs most commonly trafficked include kidneys, livers, and corneas, though nearly any organ can be trafficked.

In many cases, organ trafficking involves a highly organized network of criminals who exploit vulnerable individuals for profit. These individuals may be coerced, deceived, or forced into selling their organs, often in exchange for money or promises of a better life. The trade is usually carried out in clandestine settings, often in countries with lax regulation or weak enforcement of medical and legal practices.

This illicit trade, while operating in the shadows, is a multi-billion-dollar industry. It flourishes in regions where there is a significant gap between the demand for organs and their legal availability. Organ trafficking presents serious health risks to both donors and recipients, as it often involves unregulated medical procedures carried out in unsafe conditions. Furthermore, the practice is driven by a web of social, political, and economic factors that make it both highly lucrative and difficult to eliminate.

THE ROOTS OF ORGAN TRAFFICKING: DEMAND AND SUPPLY MISMATCH

The origins of organ trafficking can be traced back to the growing demand for organ transplants coupled with the scarcity of legally available organs. According to the World Health Organization (WHO), there are more than 130,000 people worldwide awaiting organ transplants at any given time. However, less than 10% of the demand is met, creating a significant gap between the number of people needing transplants and the number of organs available for donation.

Several factors contribute to the global shortage of organs, including:

1 Lack of Organ Donation Culture: In many countries, there is a general reluctance to donate organs. Cultural, religious, and personal beliefs often deter individuals from registering as organ donors. As a result, organ donation rates remain low, exacerbating the global shortage.

2 Strict Regulations: While many countries have established ethical guidelines and strict regulations for organ donation, these regulations often lead to an imbalance between supply and demand. Although organ donation is voluntary in most countries, the strict ethical standards governing who can donate, as well as the restrictions on how organs are allocated, create barriers to increasing supply.

3 Waiting Lists: As the demand for organ transplants continues to outstrip the supply, individuals are often placed on long waiting lists for organs. In many cases, people are forced to wait years for a suitable donor organ. In some countries, this wait can lead individuals to seek alternative, and often illegal, means of obtaining an organ.

THE ANATOMY OF ORGAN TRAFFICKING

Organ trafficking is a complex and clandestine practice that involves multiple actors, from the donors to the recipients, intermediaries, and medical professionals who may be complicit in the process. The market operates in a range of countries, from those with weak legal frameworks to those with highly advanced medical infrastructure. The process of organ trafficking typically follows a specific pattern:

1 Recruitment of Organ Donors: Traffickers often prey on vulnerable populations, including the poor, marginalized communities, and those living in conflict zones. These individuals are frequently promised large sums of money in exchange for selling one of their kidneys or other organs. They may be coerced or manipulated into the trade with false promises, such as the assurance of life-changing sums of money or medical treatment.

2 Transportation and Exploitation: Once individuals agree to sell their organs, they are often transported to a different country where they undergo surgery in unsafe, unregulated conditions. Many donors are told that they will be provided with medical care, but in reality, they are subjected to dangerous procedures without proper post-operative care.

3 The Role of Middlemen: Middlemen play a critical role in facilitating organ trafficking. These individuals act as intermediaries between the organ donors, recipients, and surgeons, organizing the entire process and profiting from the trade. They may be involved in recruiting donors, negotiating prices, arranging travel and medical logistics, and handling payments.

4 The Transplant Surgery: The organs are usually removed by unscrupulous medical professionals who may work in unregistered or illegal clinics. These surgeries often take place in secret, without proper medical protocols or post-operative care. This increases the risk of complications, infections, and death for the donors. The recipients, who may come from wealthier backgrounds, are often unaware of the illegal nature of the transaction.

5 Organ Sale and Distribution: Once the organ is harvested, it is sold to the highest bidder. The recipients are often desperate individuals who cannot afford the legal costs associated with organ transplants, or those who are willing to bypass the long waiting lists. The black market for organs can be extensive, with organ prices varying widely depending on location, the type of organ, and the level of demand.

THE COUNTRIES MOST AFFECTED BY ORGAN TRAFFICKING

Organ trafficking is not confined to any one region or country. It is a global issue, but certain countries are more vulnerable to the trade due to factors such as poverty, weak legal systems, political instability, or insufficient medical oversight. Some of the most affected regions include:

1 India: India has long been one of the countries most affected by organ trafficking, largely due to the high demand for organs and a significant gap between organ supply and need. The country has seen a rise in illegal kidney transplants, particularly in rural areas where poor individuals are targeted by traffickers. In the past, organized crime syndicates operated illegal transplant centers, often without the knowledge or consent of the recipients.

2 China: China is known for its controversial organ transplant practices, with reports of organs being harvested from executed prisoners. While the country has made efforts to reform its organ donation system, concerns about the ethical implications of forced organ harvesting persist. China has also been accused of participating in organ trafficking, particularly in relation to prisoners of conscience, such as the Falun Gong practitioners.

3 Middle East: In certain countries in the Middle East, organ trafficking has been reported to take place, particularly in regions with wealthy populations and significant economic disparities. Some reports indicate that individuals from poorer countries are recruited to donate organs to wealthy recipients, often under duress or false pretenses.

4 Eastern Europe and Central Asia: Countries in Eastern Europe and Central Asia, including Moldova, Kazakhstan, and Turkey, have been implicated in the illegal trade of human organs. The combination of poverty, corruption, and a lack of effective law enforcement has made these regions hotspots for organ trafficking. Some individuals in these regions are promised large sums of money in exchange for selling their organs, with little understanding of the long-term health risks.

5 Africa: In sub-Saharan Africa, organ trafficking has been reported as a growing issue. Poor communities, particularly in countries like Nigeria and South Africa, are targeted by traffickers who promise quick cash for the sale of kidneys or other organs. The lack of access to proper healthcare and the prevalence of economic hardship in these regions make them vulnerable to exploitation by criminals operating in the organ trade.

THE HEALTH AND ETHICAL IMPLICATIONS OF ORGAN TRAFFICKING

The consequences of organ trafficking are severe, both for the victims who are coerced or exploited into selling their organs and for the recipients who receive these illegally obtained organs. The health risks for both donors and recipients are significant.

Health Risks for Organ Donors

1 Physical Harm: The surgeries involved in organ trafficking are often performed in unsanitary conditions, without proper medical oversight or skilled professionals. The removal of organs, particularly kidneys, can result in severe complications, such as infections, bleeding, and even death. Donors may suffer from long-term physical ailments, including kidney failure, chronic pain, and loss of physical function.

2 Psychological Trauma: Victims of organ trafficking often experience psychological trauma as a result of being coerced, exploited, or deceived. Many donors report feeling regret, shame, and guilt, particularly if they were misled about the risks or the amount of money they would receive.

3 Post-Operative Care Deficiency: In many cases, donors do not receive adequate post-operative care, leading to complications such as infections or organ rejection. Without proper medical attention, donors are at risk of suffering permanent damage to their health.

ETHICAL AND SOCIAL CONCERNS

Organ trafficking raises serious ethical concerns, particularly regarding the exploitation of vulnerable populations. It preys on individuals who are economically disadvantaged or marginalized, manipulating their desperation to create a highly profitable trade. The commodification of human organs is also seen as a violation of human dignity, as it reduces individuals to mere suppliers of body parts.

The recipients of trafficked organs also face ethical questions, as they may be complicit in a system that exploits the poor and vulnerable. While these recipients may be in desperate need of a transplant, their actions contribute to the perpetuation of the illegal organ trade.

INTERNATIONAL EFFORTS TO COMBAT ORGAN TRAFFICKING

The global rise of organ trafficking has led to significant international efforts to address the issue. Several organizations, governments, and advocacy groups have worked to combat the illegal trade in human organs and improve the ethical standards surrounding organ transplantation.

1 The World Health Organization (WHO): The WHO has been at the forefront of efforts to combat organ trafficking, publishing guidelines and reports on the issue. The organization has emphasized the importance of legal and ethical organ donation systems, calling for international cooperation to eliminate the black market for human organs.

2 The Declaration of Istanbul: In 2008, the Declaration of Istanbul was adopted by a group of medical professionals and transplant experts. The declaration aims to promote ethical practices in organ transplantation and to combat the trafficking and sale of human organs. It calls for stronger regulatory frameworks and more equitable access to transplantation services.

3 National Legislation: Many countries have introduced laws and regulations to combat organ trafficking. For example, India passed the Transplantation of Human Organs Act in 1994, which makes it illegal to sell or purchase human organs. Similarly, the United States has passed laws that criminalize organ trafficking, including the National Organ Transplant Act, which bans the sale of organs.

4 Public Awareness and Education: Non-governmental organizations (NGOs) and advocacy groups have played a critical role in raising awareness about organ trafficking. These organizations educate the public about the risks and ethical concerns associated with organ trafficking and work to empower vulnerable communities with information about their rights.

5 International Cooperation: Global collaboration has been vital in tackling organ trafficking. Interpol, the United Nations, and other international bodies have worked together to coordinate efforts to combat the trade in human organs. These organizations support law enforcement agencies in tracking and apprehending traffickers and raising awareness about the issue.

CONCLUSION: THE ONGOING STRUGGLE AGAINST ORGAN TRAFFICKING

Organ trafficking remains one of the most serious human rights challenges of the modern age. It is driven by a combination of factors, including the global shortage of organs for transplant, widespread poverty, and a lack of effective legal and regulatory frameworks. While efforts have been made at the international, national, and grassroots levels to address this issue, much work remains to be done.

To truly combat organ trafficking, it is essential to build stronger legal systems, improve access to ethical organ donation and transplant services, and address the social and economic conditions that make vulnerable populations susceptible to exploitation. Only by addressing these underlying factors can the illegal trade in human organs be eradicated and replaced by fair, equitable, and transparent systems for organ donation and transplantation.

CHAPTER 16
THE HOLOCAUST
THE SYSTEMATIC MURDER OF SIX MILLION JEWS

Awaiting Selection

THE RISE OF NAZI IDEOLOGY

The story of the Holocaust begins long before the gas chambers, long before the horrors of Auschwitz, and long before the death marches. It begins in the aftermath of World War I, during a time of intense hardship in Germany. The Treaty of Versailles, which formally ended the war, had imposed crippling reparations on the country, and Germany was in economic ruin. Hyperinflation, widespread unemployment, and a sense of national humiliation created a fertile ground for extreme ideologies.

Among the many factions vying for control in this chaos, the National Socialist German Workers' Party (NSDAP), led by Adolf Hitler, emerged as the most radical. Hitler's speeches, filled with venomous rhetoric against Jews, Communists, and others he deemed "undesirable," struck a chord with a population that felt betrayed and vulnerable. His vision of a racially pure Aryan state resonated with those who were desperate for a sense of pride and national identity.

But Hitler's rise to power wasn't inevitable. It was the result of meticulous planning, manipulation of public opinion, and an increasingly brutal crackdown on political opponents. With the support of powerful figures like Heinrich Himmler, Joseph Goebbels, and others, Hitler was appointed Chancellor of Germany in January 1933. This was the beginning of a regime that would enact policies of racial discrimination, persecution, and ultimately genocide on an unprecedented scale.

The idea of "racial purity" was central to Nazi ideology, and Jews were cast as the primary enemy. The Jews were blamed for Germany's defeat in World War I and for the economic and social problems of the Weimar Republic. Hitler's anti-Semitic views were not new; they had been part of European history for centuries. But the Nazis took them to a terrifying extreme, making them a cornerstone of their vision for the future.

THE IMPLEMENTATION OF ANTI-SEMITIC LAWS AND PROPAGANDA

Once in power, the Nazi regime wasted no time in enacting laws that discriminated against Jews. The Nuremberg Laws of 1935 were the legal foundation for systemic anti-Semitic policies. These laws prohibited Jews from marrying non-Jews, banned them from holding public office, and restricted their participation in many professions. They also required Jews to wear yellow Star of David badges to identify themselves in public.

The propaganda machine, led by Joseph Goebbels, worked tirelessly to spread Nazi ideology. Films, posters, and rallies portrayed Jews as subhuman and dangerous. The famous 1935 Nazi film *The Eternal Jew* depicted Jews as vermin and parasites. In this atmosphere of hatred, acts of violence against Jews became increasingly common. Jewish businesses were boycotted, synagogues were burned, and Jews were publicly humiliated.

In 1938, the situation took a more violent turn with Kristallnacht, or the Night of Broken Glass. On November 9 and 10, 1938, mobs across Germany attacked Jewish homes, businesses, and synagogues. The streets were littered with broken glass, and dozens of Jews were killed. This violent pogrom marked the beginning of a more overt campaign of violence and intimidation against Jews.

THE ROAD TO THE FINAL SOLUTION

As Nazi power expanded across Europe, so too did their anti-Semitic policies. The invasion of Poland in 1939 marked the beginning of a broader war in Europe, but it also heralded a new phase in the treatment of Jews. In the occupied territories, Jews were forced into ghettos, overcrowded and unsanitary districts where they were isolated from the rest of society. Starvation, disease, and brutal treatment were rampant in these ghettos, but this was only the beginning.

In the early 1940s, the Nazis began to implement what would later be called the "Final Solution"—the systematic extermination of Jews. Initially, the Nazis tried to address the "Jewish Question" through forced emigration, but this was deemed insufficient. As the war escalated, and Nazi troops moved into the Soviet Union, the scale of the mass murder grew. Mobile killing units, called Einsatzgruppen, followed behind the advancing German army, rounding up Jews and executing them in mass shootings.

THE MECHANISM OF MASS MURDER: THE CONCENTRATION CAMPS

By the time the Nazis had consolidated their control over most of Europe, they had moved beyond discrimination and violent persecution to systematically orchestrating mass murder. The scale of their efforts to exterminate Jews and other "undesirables" was chillingly organized, demonstrating a level of brutality that defied imagination.

The first concentration camps were established in the early 1930s, intended for political opponents of the Nazi regime. However, as Nazi ideology evolved, the camps began to serve a darker purpose: the suppression, enslavement, and eventual destruction of entire populations. As the war expanded across Europe, the Nazis transformed these camps into death factories where millions of innocent lives would be extinguished in horrific ways.

The creation of the death camps was a decisive step toward the "Final Solution." The Nazis aimed not only to isolate and dehumanize Jews but to physically annihilate them. The architecture of death was purpose-built in these camps, designed for efficiency in the mass killing of human beings.

One of the most infamous camps was Auschwitz-Birkenau, a site where over a million Jews were murdered, along with hundreds of thousands of Roma, disabled individuals, and Polish resistance fighters. Auschwitz was a multifunctional complex, with labor camps, medical experimentation centers, and extermination facilities all located within its bounds.

The killing process in Auschwitz was disturbingly methodical. Upon arrival, prisoners were immediately divided into groups, with the elderly, women, children, and those who appeared unfit for labor sent directly to the gas chambers. In many cases, the deception began at the train station, where newly arrived prisoners were told that they were simply going to take a shower or undergo medical treatment. The gas chambers, disguised as shower facilities, could accommodate hundreds of people at a time. Zyclon B, a poisonous gas, was used to murder the prisoners. The bodies were then burned in crematoriums or disposed of in mass graves.

In Treblinka, another notorious extermination camp, the killing was equally systematic. The Nazis utilized gas chambers in what was referred to as the "Operation Reinhard" campaign, which aimed to exterminate Jews from the General Government region of occupied Poland. Between 1942 and 1943, nearly 900,000 Jews were murdered in Treblinka. Unlike Auschwitz, Treblinka was purely an extermination camp, with no labor or resettlement plans for its prisoners. The process was designed to be swift and anonymous, with trains arriving daily, unloading people into gas chambers disguised as showers, and the bodies quickly incinerated.

The methods of murder extended beyond gas chambers. Thousands of Jews and others were shot in mass executions, left to die in pits or shot in the back of the head by Nazi soldiers. This was especially common in the East, where the Einsatzgruppen (mobile killing units) followed the advancing Wehrmacht, murdering Jews, Communists, intellectuals, and anyone suspected of opposing Nazi rule. In the wake of these killings, the bodies were often piled in mass graves, left unburied or partially burned to hide the evidence. In many cases, the victims' families were forced to dig the graves for their loved ones before being shot themselves.

The brutal treatment of prisoners in the camps went beyond mass executions. Inmates were subjected to medical experimentation, conducted by notorious figures like Dr. Josef Mengele, a physician at Auschwitz. Mengele, known as the

"Angel of Death," conducted horrifying experiments on twins, individuals with disabilities, and anyone else he deemed a subject of study. These experiments were often cruel and inhumane, with no regard for the victims' health or safety.

But even in the midst of this horror, the human spirit did not break entirely. Some prisoners managed to resist, defying their captors in any way they could. Though most resistance movements within the camps were small and ultimately crushed, they offered a defiant stand against the systematic cruelty.

SURVIVOR TESTIMONIES AND RESISTANCE MOVEMENTS

The Holocaust was not only a time of unimaginable suffering but also a time when acts of extraordinary courage occurred. Resistance movements existed both inside the ghettos and in the concentration camps, despite the overwhelming odds stacked against them. One of the most well-known acts of resistance took place in the Warsaw Ghetto, where, in 1943, Jewish insurgents fought back against Nazi forces in a violent uprising. Though the insurgents were vastly outnumbered, they managed to inflict casualties on the Germans, delaying their plans and showing that even in the face of certain death, resistance was possible.

Some resistance movements were small and localized, while others were more organized. In Auschwitz, a group of prisoners, known as the Sonderkommando, who were forced to work in the gas chambers and crematoria, staged an uprising in 1944. Armed with smuggled weapons, the prisoners managed to kill a few guards and destroy one of the crematoriums. While the uprising was quickly suppressed, it was a powerful symbol of defiance in the face of nearly insurmountable adversity.

In addition to those who fought back, there were individuals like Oskar Schindler who acted out of a sense of moral duty, risking their lives to save others. Schindler, a German businessman, initially joined the Nazi Party, but his conscience led him to protect over 1,200 Jewish workers by employing them in his factories. His efforts were not limited to providing them with work but included bribing Nazi officials and even orchestrating their relocation to safer areas when needed. Schindler's story is one of the few tales of salvation in the midst of such darkness, and his efforts have been immortalized in books and films, reminding us of the power of individual action during times of unspeakable evil.

For the survivors, the trauma was not just physical but psychological. Many were forced to witness the deaths of their families and friends, and the horrors they experienced never left them. The psychological scars of the Holocaust continue to haunt survivors, their families, and the descendants of those who perished. Survivor testimony became an essential part of preserving the memory of the Holocaust, as the survivors were often the only ones who could bear witness to the horrors they had endured. Through books, speeches, and interviews, survivors became the human face of the tragedy, helping to ensure that the world would never forget.

LIBERATION AND AFTERMATH

As the war came to an end, the Allies liberated the remaining concentration camps in 1945. The sight of the survivors, weak and emaciated, was a stark contrast to the thriving, militaristic war machine the Nazis had once projected. But liberation came with its own challenges. The survivors, many of whom had lost entire families, returned to devastated cities and towns. Their homes and lives had been destroyed, and their identity had been stripped away. The emotional scars, the loss of family and community, were often as hard to overcome as the physical trauma.

For those who survived, the world after the Holocaust was unrecognizable. In addition to the massive loss of life, the post-war landscape was shaped by the refugee crisis. Hundreds of thousands of Jews had been displaced from their homes, unable to return to their countries of origin, and many sought refuge in countries like the United States, Israel, and Canada. The establishment of the State of Israel in 1948 became a pivotal moment for many Holocaust survivors, offering a homeland where Jews could live free from persecution.

In the aftermath, the Nuremberg Trials became an essential part of the process of reckoning with the atrocities of the Holocaust. Nazi leaders and high-ranking officials were tried for war crimes, crimes against humanity, and genocide. The trials were instrumental in establishing the principle that individuals could be held accountable for crimes against humanity, regardless of their position in a government or military hierarchy. Some of the most infamous perpetrators, like Hermann Göring and Rudolf Hess, were convicted and sentenced to death or imprisonment. However, many Nazi officers and collaborators escaped justice, some fleeing to countries in South America or hiding under false identities.

While the trials represented a form of justice, the scars of the Holocaust could never truly be healed through legal means. Survivors had to live with the memories of their loved ones' deaths, the brutality they experienced, and the trauma of witnessing the unimaginable. For many, the emotional toll was lifelong, and their experiences were often dismissed or minimized in the early years after the war.

THE BROADER IMPACT: INTERNATIONAL RESPONSES AND THE FIGHT FOR JUSTICE

While the Holocaust marked one of the darkest periods of human history, its aftermath catalyzed global reflection and action that reshaped international law and human rights. The full extent of the horrors perpetrated by the Nazi regime didn't become entirely known to the global community until the war ended, when the Allied forces liberated the concentration and extermination camps. The images of emaciated survivors, piles of corpses, and the evidence of mass murder left the world in shock.

In the years immediately following World War II, the international community was forced to confront the unimaginable scale of the genocide. In response to the atrocities, the Nuremberg Trials were held to bring Nazi war criminals to justice. The trials were a significant moment in the development of international law, as they established the principle that individuals, rather than just states, could be held accountable for war crimes and crimes against humanity.

The Nuremberg Trials became a model for future war crimes trials, but they also revealed the limitations and challenges of international justice. Many high-ranking Nazis were executed or imprisoned, but numerous others were never apprehended. Some, like Adolf Eichmann, the architect of the Final Solution, escaped to South America, where they lived in hiding for years before being captured. These evasion efforts revealed the disturbing fact that many people who had committed war crimes were able to escape justice, leading to frustration among the global community.

In addition to the trials, the Holocaust sparked a series of reforms in the international community, particularly in the realm of human rights. In 1948, the United Nations adopted the Universal Declaration of Human Rights, a monumental document that sought to safeguard the dignity and rights of all human beings, irrespective of nationality, ethnicity, or religion. This was partly a response to the shocking disregard for human life and dignity demonstrated during the Holocaust.

One of the most significant outcomes was the establishment of the State of Israel in 1948, which provided a safe haven for Jewish survivors of the Holocaust. The creation of Israel was not only a response to centuries of anti-Semitism but also a recognition of the need for a Jewish homeland where survivors could rebuild their lives and ensure the survival of Jewish culture, history, and identity. For many Holocaust survivors, however, the creation of Israel was both a beacon of hope and a bittersweet reminder of the immense loss they had suffered.

THE ROLE OF MEMORY: PRESERVING THE HOLOCAUST IN MODERN TIMES

As time has passed, the memory of the Holocaust has taken on an increasingly important role in shaping global consciousness. For the survivors and their families, the trauma is not just a personal burden; it is a collective one. Their stories are intertwined with the history of the Jewish people and the history of humanity itself. Efforts to preserve the memory of the Holocaust have become integral to educating future generations and ensuring that such horrors are never repeated.

Numerous Holocaust museums and memorials have been established around the world, providing spaces for reflection, education, and remembrance. The United States Holocaust Memorial Museum in Washington, D.C., is one of the most prominent examples of such institutions, dedicated to documenting the atrocities of the Holocaust and teaching future generations about the dangers of intolerance and hatred. Museums in Germany, Poland, and Israel also play critical roles in preserving the history of the Holocaust, ensuring that the lessons of this genocide are never forgotten.

In addition to physical memorials, modern technology has provided new ways to preserve survivor testimonies. Documentaries, books, and digital archives have allowed the voices of survivors to reach a broader audience than ever before. The Shoah Foundation, founded by filmmaker Steven Spielberg after the success of his film *Schindler's List*, has been at the forefront of recording and preserving survivor testimonies. These testimonies provide a vivid, firsthand account of life before, during, and after the Holocaust, preserving personal stories of resilience and loss for future generations.

Educational programs focused on the Holocaust have expanded in schools and universities worldwide, emphasizing the importance of tolerance, human rights, and the dangers of prejudice. Many countries have implemented Holocaust education as part of their school curricula, ensuring that young people learn about this dark chapter in history and understand its relevance to today's world.

However, the passage of time and the diminishing number of survivors presents a unique challenge. As the Holocaust recedes into the past, the challenge of ensuring its history is passed on becomes more urgent. With fewer living witnesses, the risk of Holocaust denial and revisionism grows. Some individuals and groups continue to downplay the scale of the genocide or promote outright denial. This phenomenon, in part fueled by political ideologies and ignorance, poses a significant threat to historical truth.

In response, Holocaust education has become an even more critical tool for combating misinformation and preserving the lessons of the past. Efforts to educate the public about the facts of the Holocaust and the dangers of anti-Semitism have grown in prominence. But combating denial is not just about historical facts; it's about preserving the memory of those who perished and ensuring that their stories remain an integral part of our collective consciousness.

THE ONGOING BATTLE: ANTI-SEMITISM AND THE RELEVANCE OF THE HOLOCAUST TODAY

In the years since the end of World War II, the world has made significant progress in many areas, but the legacy of the Holocaust continues to reverberate in the ongoing battle against hatred, prejudice, and bigotry. One of the most persistent threats in this regard is anti-Semitism, a form of hatred that fueled the Holocaust and continues to target Jewish communities worldwide.

While much progress has been made since the 1940s, anti-Semitism remains a significant problem in many parts of the world. It takes many forms, from overt violence and vandalism to more subtle forms of discrimination and exclusion. In recent years, there has been a disturbing rise in anti-Semitic incidents, particularly in Europe, where attacks on Jewish individuals, synagogues, and institutions have become more frequent. This resurgence of anti-Semitism is a stark reminder that the fight against hatred is ongoing and requires vigilance and action.

The Holocaust, in many ways, serves as both a warning and a call to action. The events of the 1930s and 1940s demonstrate the catastrophic consequences of unchecked hatred, intolerance, and racism. It is a chilling reminder of how easily dehumanization can turn into violence, and how the world can stand by while atrocities are committed. The memory of the Holocaust compels us to stand against all forms of hatred, wherever they appear, and to speak out against injustice, no matter how small or seemingly insignificant.

Many survivors and their families continue to speak out, not only to preserve the memory of the Holocaust but to prevent future atrocities. Their testimonies have become more important than ever, offering a firsthand account of the horrors of the Holocaust and the lessons we must learn from it. For these survivors, telling their stories is not just an act of remembrance but an act of resistance against the forces of hate.

At the same time, Holocaust survivors have emphasized the importance of tolerance, kindness, and understanding, values that should shape our societies. They stress the need for empathy and the importance of recognizing our shared humanity. The ultimate lesson of the Holocaust is not just that such evil must never happen again but that we, as individuals and as a global community, must actively work to make the world a better, more compassionate place.

CONCLUSION: THE ENDURING LEGACY OF THE HOLOCAUST

The Holocaust remains one of the most profound and painful events in human history, and its legacy continues to shape our world in countless ways. It is a reminder of the depths of cruelty and barbarity that humans are capable of, but it is also a testament to the resilience of the human spirit. The survivors, the families of the victims, and those who continue to honor their memory have shown us the importance of hope, strength, and determination in the face of overwhelming adversity.

The lessons of the Holocaust extend far beyond the Jewish people; they apply to all of humanity. The Holocaust teaches us the dangers of indifference, the consequences of unchecked hatred, and the imperative to defend human dignity, regardless of race, religion, or background. It is a call to recognize our shared humanity and a plea for justice, peace, and reconciliation.

In the years to come, as the last survivors of the Holocaust pass on, the responsibility of keeping their stories alive falls to the rest of us. We must ensure that the memory of the Holocaust is preserved, that the lessons are passed down, and that future generations understand the dangers of prejudice, discrimination, and hatred. The Holocaust is not just a part of the past —it is a crucial lesson for the present and the future.

The legacy of the Holocaust lives on not only in museums and memorials but in the fight for justice, equality, and human rights. As long as we continue to remember, we can ensure that the victims are not forgotten, and that the darkness of the past never repeats itself.

CHAPTER 17
THE DISAPPEARANCE OF FLIGHT MH370
UNSOLVED AVIATION MYSTERY

Flight MH 370 Plane On An Earlier Flight

On March 8, 2014, Malaysia Airlines Flight MH370, a Boeing 777-200ER, took off from Kuala Lumpur International Airport, bound for Beijing Capital International Airport. The flight carried 227 passengers and 12 crew members, all of whom were presumed to be on a routine flight. However, within less than an hour after takeoff, MH370 inexplicably vanished from radar, and what followed was one of the most baffling and widely publicized aviation mysteries of the 21st century. The disappearance of MH370 triggered an unprecedented search operation, involved dozens of countries, and left the world grappling with questions that remain largely unanswered.

THE LAST MOMENTS OF FLIGHT MH370

On March 8, 2014, Malaysia Airlines Flight MH370 departed from Kuala Lumpur at 12:41 AM local time. The aircraft was en route to Beijing, a flight that typically takes about six and a half hours. Flight MH370 was carrying 227 passengers, including citizens from over a dozen countries, and 12 crew members. The aircraft, a Boeing 777-200ER, had a good safety record and had completed 53,000 flight hours without major incidents.

The aircraft took off without any unusual signs or technical difficulties, and the flight's progress was initially smooth. However, the events that followed would send shockwaves around the world.

THE LOSS OF CONTACT

Approximately 38 minutes after takeoff, at 1:19 AM, the flight's final transmission to air traffic control was made. The aircraft's communication system, known as the Aircraft Communications Addressing and Reporting System (ACARS), sent a routine data transmission about the flight's progress. The pilot, Captain Zaharie Ahmad Shah, communicated with air traffic control at 1:19 AM, saying, "Good night, Malaysian three-seven-zero," marking the last known words of the flight. This transmission occurred as the aircraft passed through Malaysia's airspace and was handed off to Vietnamese air traffic controllers.

At 1:21 AM, air traffic control lost contact with the aircraft. Initially, it was assumed that the plane had simply gone out of range. However, no distress signals were received from the aircraft, and no alarms or indications of problems were reported by the crew.

THE RADAR DATA AND THE MYSTERIOUS TURN

At 2:15 AM, more than an hour after losing contact, military radar data revealed something astonishing. The aircraft had made a sharp, deliberate turn to the west, taking it off course from its original path to Beijing. The aircraft flew back across the Malaysian Peninsula, crossing the Gulf of Thailand, and headed south over the Malay Peninsula toward the Indian Ocean.

This turn was not consistent with a mechanical failure or an accident, and the aircraft's autopilot seemed to be engaged.

The flight's last known position was near the southern tip of the Malay Peninsula, and it was now on a path that would lead it toward the remote areas of the Indian Ocean, far from any major landmasses. The fact that the aircraft had turned around and was flying in the opposite direction of its intended route raised serious questions.

THE INABILITY TO TRACK THE AIRCRAFT

The absence of further communications, combined with the plane's unexpected course change, meant that authorities were left in a state of confusion. The lack of reliable tracking and the remote area the plane was headed to meant that it would be difficult to find the aircraft if it had crashed or made an emergency landing.

In addition to the ACARS data, which could have provided crucial information about the aircraft's systems, the aircraft's transponder—an important piece of equipment that broadcasts the plane's location to radar stations—was turned off. This created an even more significant challenge for investigators, as the transponder is key to determining the aircraft's exact position in real time. The failure to receive any further updates from the plane left aviation authorities with very little to go on.

THE INITIAL SEARCH EFFORTS

As soon as the aircraft's disappearance was realized, search operations were launched. The initial search area focused on the region near the last known position of the aircraft, in the South China Sea, where authorities feared the plane may have crashed. More than 40 ships, aircraft, and personnel were deployed to search the area, but no trace of the aircraft was found.

A few days after the disappearance, Malaysian authorities broadened the search area after analysis of satellite data revealed that the aircraft may have continued flying for several hours after losing contact with air traffic control. The new data suggested that MH370 could have traveled far off course, heading into the remote areas of the southern Indian Ocean.

THE INVOLVEMENT OF INTERNATIONAL AGENCIES

As the search expanded, the involvement of multiple countries became critical. Australia, which had experience with large-scale search operations, became the lead agency in coordinating the search in the southern Indian Ocean. The Australian Transport Safety Bureau (ATSB) was tasked with overseeing the search operations, and a team of experts from around the world, including representatives from Malaysia, the United States, the United Kingdom, China, and several other countries, joined the effort.

The search was conducted in multiple phases, initially focusing on a vast area that stretched across the Indian Ocean. Search crews scoured the area using a combination of surface vessels, aircraft, and underwater drones in the hope of finding wreckage or other clues.

THE ROLE OF SATELLITE DATA: THE "HANDSHAKE"

One of the most critical pieces of evidence came from a method of satellite communication known as "handshakes." These handshakes were a series of automated communications between the aircraft and a satellite ground station. After the plane lost radar contact, the satellite continued to receive "pings" from the plane, which provided investigators with important clues about the aircraft's flight path.

The satellite data showed that after the final communication at 1:19 AM, MH370 continued flying for several more hours. This information allowed investigators to narrow the potential crash site down to a 60,000-square-kilometer area of the southern Indian Ocean, a region that is both vast and remote, making the search incredibly difficult.

THEORIES ON THE DISAPPEARANCE

As the search continued without finding any wreckage, theories about the disappearance of MH370 began to emerge. These ranged from technical malfunctions to more sinister explanations. Below are some of the major theories that have been proposed:

Mechanical Failure

One possibility is that MH370 experienced a sudden mechanical failure, such as an explosive decompression or an engine malfunction, which incapacitated the crew and left the plane flying on autopilot until it ran out of fuel and crashed. However, this theory was dismissed by many experts, as there was no indication of any distress calls or emergencies from the crew prior to the disappearance.

Hijacking or Terrorism

Another theory that gained attention was the possibility of a hijacking or terrorist attack. Some speculated that the plane was hijacked by individuals on board and flown off course, while others suggested that the aircraft might have been targeted for reasons related to international terrorism. However, after extensive investigation, no credible evidence surfaced linking the flight to terrorism, and there were no claims of responsibility from any terrorist group.

Pilot Involvement

One of the most widely discussed theories was that of pilot involvement. Captain Zaharie Ahmad Shah, the pilot of MH370, was considered a highly experienced and competent aviator. However, investigators discovered that he had created a flight simulation on his home computer in the weeks leading up to the disappearance, which included a route that mirrored the flight path of MH370's last known trajectory.

Some speculated that Captain Zaharie might have deliberately diverted the plane, possibly for personal or political reasons. However, no clear motive was ever established, and the theory remains highly controversial. Additionally, the co-pilot, Fariq Abdul Hamid, was also found to have no involvement in any form of criminal activity.

THE "REMOTE LOCATION" THEORY: THE SOUTHERN INDIAN OCEAN

The southern Indian Ocean became the focal point of the search after the satellite data indicated that the aircraft had traveled in that direction. Given the vastness of the area and the depth of the ocean, finding wreckage in such a location was always going to be a difficult task. Despite extensive efforts to locate the aircraft, the remote location and unpredictable ocean currents made it nearly impossible to search effectively.

THE DISCOVERY OF WRECKAGE

In 2015, more than a year after the aircraft disappeared, a piece of MH370's wing—known as a flaperon—was found washed up on the shores of Réunion Island, located in the western Indian Ocean. The discovery of this piece of wreckage confirmed that MH370 had crashed into the ocean, but it did little to explain the reasons behind the disappearance or where the aircraft might have gone down.

Over the next few years, additional pieces of debris, including parts of the fuselage and other wing components, were found washed up on the shores of various islands along the Indian Ocean, from Mozambique to Tanzania. While these discoveries provided some confirmation that the aircraft had ended its journey in the ocean, they did little to solve the mystery of what happened to the plane in the moments before it disappeared.

THE FORMAL END OF THE SEARCH

In 2018, after years of fruitless searching and the expenditure of hundreds of millions of dollars, the Australian government officially announced the suspension of the search for MH370. The search had covered over 120,000 square kilometers of the southern Indian Ocean, but no further wreckage was found, and the reasons behind the aircraft's disappearance remained unclear.

However, the official end of the search did not mark the end of the quest for answers. The families of the passengers and crew members on board MH370 continue to demand further investigation, and the mystery of the missing plane remains a topic of public interest and speculation.

THEORIES ON WHAT HAPPENED: THE NEED FOR CLOSURE

As of now, the disappearance of MH370 remains one of the greatest unsolved mysteries in aviation history. While the satellite "handshakes" suggest that the plane flew for hours after losing radar contact, the reasons for the deviation from its flight path, the pilot's actions, and the failure of the aircraft's communication systems remain unanswered.

The tragedy of MH370 has left an indelible mark on the world's collective consciousness. Families continue to seek closure, investigators continue to probe for answers, and the aviation community remains on alert, working to ensure that such an event never happens again.

CONCLUSION: THE LEGACY OF FLIGHT MH370

The disappearance of Malaysia Airlines Flight MH370 is a tragedy that has profoundly impacted the world. The search for answers, spanning over a decade, has involved numerous governments, agencies, and experts, but the true cause of the plane's disappearance remains a mystery.

While the search has officially concluded, the unanswered questions and the search for closure continue. The story of MH370 is a reminder of the uncertainties that still exist in modern aviation, as well as the resilience of those who continue to seek the truth.

For the families and loved ones of those on board MH370, the hope for answers

CHAPTER 18
THE 2014 JP MORGAN CHASE BANK HACKING
83 MILLION VICTIMS

J P Morgan Chase HQ Building

In 2014, one of the most significant cybersecurity breaches in history took place when JPMorgan Chase Bank, the largest bank in the United States and one of the biggest financial institutions in the world, fell victim to a massive cyber attack. The hack compromised the personal and financial data of over 76 million households and 7 million small businesses, making it one of the largest and most damaging cyberattacks on a financial institution in history. This breach raised serious questions about the security measures at major financial institutions, the evolving nature of cyber threats, and the ability of banks to protect sensitive customer information in the digital age.

THE BACKGROUND OF JPMORGAN CHASE BANK

JPMorgan Chase & Co. is one of the oldest and largest financial institutions in the world. It operates in over 60 countries and provides a wide range of services, including investment banking, asset management, and private banking. With more than $2 trillion in assets, JPMorgan Chase serves millions of customers and holds vast amounts of sensitive financial data, making it an attractive target for cybercriminals.

In 2014, JPMorgan Chase was well aware of the cybersecurity risks it faced, given the ever-evolving nature of cybercrime. The bank had invested heavily in security measures, including advanced encryption, firewalls, and regular security audits. However, despite these efforts, hackers were able to infiltrate the bank's network, compromising vast amounts of customer information.

THE DISCOVERY OF THE HACK

The breach came to light in late July 2014, although the attack itself was believed to have started as early as June 2014. The bank's cybersecurity team discovered unusual activity in its computer systems, which prompted an investigation. It was later revealed that the attack had compromised the bank's internal networks, specifically the part of the network that handles the bank's online banking services.

The hackers were able to access an alarming amount of sensitive data, including customer names, addresses, phone numbers, email addresses, and internal bank records. However, the bank's payment systems, account passwords, and other more sensitive financial data were not compromised in the breach. Although the attack was large-scale and extensive, it did not have a direct impact on the ability of JPMorgan Chase's customers to conduct financial transactions.

While the bank's systems were able to detect the breach relatively quickly, the damage had already been done. The attackers had access to the bank's systems for several months before the breach was discovered, and it was believed that they were able to maintain a foothold in the network during this period. The scale and duration of the attack made it one of the most serious breaches of data security ever to be disclosed in the banking sector.

THE METHODS OF THE ATTACK

The exact methods used by the hackers to infiltrate JPMorgan Chase's systems have been the subject of much investigation and speculation. While many of the specifics remain classified, investigators have uncovered several key details about how the attack was carried out.

THE INITIAL BREACH: EXPLOITING A VULNERABILITY

The attack began with the exploitation of a vulnerability in the bank's network. According to reports, the hackers initially gained access through an employee's compromised account. It is believed that the attackers used a simple phishing attack to gain the credentials of one of the bank's employees, which allowed them to bypass some of the bank's security measures. This method is particularly effective because it exploits human error rather than technical vulnerabilities in software.

Once the hackers obtained the credentials, they were able to gain access to the bank's network and move laterally, exploring different areas of the system. They used sophisticated techniques to avoid detection and maintained access to JPMorgan Chase's internal systems for months, extracting data without triggering alarms.

The Use of a Botnet

A key part of the attack involved the use of a botnet, a network of infected computers that can be controlled remotely by cybercriminals. The botnet allowed the attackers to maintain access to JPMorgan Chase's systems and use the bank's computing power to conduct their attack. By using a botnet, the hackers were able to mask their activity and evade detection by the bank's cybersecurity team.

The botnet also helped the attackers maintain persistence in the system, which is why they were able to remain in the bank's network for so long without being discovered. The botnet allowed them to launch attacks and exfiltrate data at will, all while staying hidden from the bank's security measures.

THE ATTACK ON SPECIFIC DATA

The primary target of the hack was the data related to JPMorgan Chase's customers. The attackers gained access to information such as:

• **Personal Information**: Names, addresses, phone numbers, and email addresses of approximately 76 million households and 7 million small businesses.

• **Account Data**: While the attackers did not gain access to sensitive financial data such as account passwords or Social Security numbers, they were able to access internal bank records, which could potentially provide further insights into customers' financial activity.

• **Internal Bank Records**: These records included proprietary information and bank operations that could potentially be used in future attacks or to exploit vulnerabilities in JPMorgan Chase's systems.

Despite the large amount of data that was compromised, the breach did not lead to any direct financial loss or fraud at the customer level. However, the fact that such a large-scale breach occurred was a major concern for both the bank and its customers.

THE RESPONSE TO THE BREACH

Once the breach was discovered, JPMorgan Chase took immediate steps to contain the attack and mitigate further damage. The bank's cybersecurity team worked quickly to identify the source of the breach and shut down any compromised access points. They also took measures to strengthen the bank's internal systems and prevent further unauthorized access.

JPMorgan Chase notified law enforcement agencies, including the FBI, which launched its own investigation into the breach. The bank also hired outside cybersecurity experts to assist with the investigation and to determine the full scope of the attack.

PUBLIC DISCLOSURE AND CUSTOMER NOTIFICATION

JPMorgan Chase did not disclose the breach to the public until September 2014, nearly two months after the hack had been discovered. This delay in disclosure drew criticism from some quarters, as customers were not immediately made aware that their personal information had been compromised. In many cases, customers were left in the dark until news of the breach broke, leading to concerns about the bank's transparency and commitment to customer protection.

When the breach was publicly revealed, JPMorgan Chase assured its customers that no financial information had been compromised. The bank also promised to provide free credit monitoring services to affected customers in an effort to mitigate potential harm from identity theft.

THE ROLE OF LAW ENFORCEMENT

The FBI launched an investigation into the attack almost immediately after JPMorgan Chase reported the breach. The investigation was complex, as the attackers had used sophisticated techniques to cover their tracks, and the scale of the breach was vast.

In the months that followed, the FBI worked with international law enforcement agencies to track down the perpetrators. The investigation ultimately revealed that the attack had been carried out by a group of Russian hackers, who were allegedly operating out of Eastern Europe. The group was later linked to a broader series of cybercrimes, including other attacks on financial institutions.

While law enforcement was able to identify the hackers and their methods, no arrests have been made in connection with the JPMorgan Chase breach. The anonymity of the internet and the international nature of cybercrime make it difficult to apprehend the individuals behind such attacks.

THE AFTERMATH: FINANCIAL AND REPUTATIONAL IMPACT

The 2014 JPMorgan Chase hack had significant consequences, both for the bank and for the broader financial industry. While the breach did not result in immediate financial losses or widespread fraud, it raised serious concerns about the security of sensitive customer data and the ability of major financial institutions to protect that data.

FINANCIAL COSTS

The financial costs of the breach were substantial. JPMorgan Chase spent millions of dollars on investigating the breach, improving its cybersecurity infrastructure, and providing credit monitoring services to affected customers. In addition to these direct costs, the bank faced legal and regulatory challenges, as lawmakers and regulators began to scrutinize the bank's handling of the breach.

While the breach did not directly lead to significant losses for JPMorgan Chase, it was a wake-up call for the banking industry as a whole. The financial sector had long been a target for cybercriminals, and the JPMorgan Chase breach demonstrated the vulnerability of even the largest and most secure institutions.

REPUTATIONAL DAMAGE

The reputational damage to JPMorgan Chase was significant. The breach raised concerns about the effectiveness of the bank's security measures and its ability to protect customer data. The delay in public disclosure also led to criticism of the bank's transparency and communication practices. Many customers were frustrated by the lack of timely information about the breach and the potential risks to their personal data.

In the aftermath of the breach, JPMorgan Chase worked to restore customer trust by implementing stronger cybersecurity measures and by improving its communication with affected customers. The bank's leadership also made efforts to reassure investors and stakeholders that the breach would not have a long-term impact on the bank's financial stability.

THE INCREASING THREAT OF CYBERCRIME

The 2014 JPMorgan Chase hack underscored the growing threat posed by cybercriminals, particularly those targeting financial institutions. As the banking sector becomes increasingly reliant on digital systems, the potential vulnerabilities that cybercriminals can exploit have increased exponentially.

The hack demonstrated that even the most sophisticated banks and financial institutions are not immune to cyberattacks. This has prompted many organizations to rethink their cybersecurity strategies and invest in more robust defense mechanisms.

A WAKE-UP CALL FOR THE FINANCIAL INDUSTRY

The breach also served as a wake-up call for the financial industry, highlighting the need for banks and other financial institutions to invest heavily in cybersecurity. In the years following the hack, financial institutions began to implement more advanced security protocols, including multi-factor authentication, encryption, and real-time monitoring.

Regulators and lawmakers have also taken a more active role in ensuring that financial institutions are adequately protecting customer data. In the United States, the Federal Reserve and other agencies have introduced new regulations and guidelines aimed at improving the cybersecurity posture of banks and ensuring that they are prepared to respond to cyber threats.

THE IMPORTANCE OF TRANSPARENCY AND COMMUNICATION

The JPMorgan Chase breach also emphasized the importance of transparency and communication in the event of a cyberattack. While the bank did take action to address the breach, its delay in publicly disclosing the attack raised questions about how companies should communicate with customers and the public during a crisis. In the future, many organizations are likely to adopt more proactive and transparent approaches to cybersecurity incidents.

CONCLUSION

The 2014 JPMorgan Chase hacking incident was a watershed moment in the world of cybersecurity and banking. The breach revealed the vulnerabilities of even the most secure financial institutions and highlighted the growing threat of cybercrime. While the breach did not lead to widespread financial loss, it raised significant concerns about the security of customer data and the effectiveness of cybersecurity measures.

In the years since the attack, JPMorgan Chase and other financial institutions have taken steps to bolster their cybersecurity defenses. The incident also led to increased scrutiny from regulators and lawmakers, who are working to ensure that banks are adequately prepared to protect sensitive customer information in the face of increasingly sophisticated cyber threats.

Ultimately, the 2014 JPMorgan Chase hack serves as a cautionary tale for organizations in all industries, reminding them of the ever-present risks posed by cybercriminals and the need for constant vigilance and investment in cybersecurity.

CHAPTER 19
THE COCAINE TRADE
TRADING IN MISERY

Cocaine King Pablo Escobar

The cocaine industry, one of the most lucrative and illicit businesses in the world, has evolved over centuries from an ancient Andean ritual to a transnational criminal enterprise. Despite widespread efforts by governments and organizations to curtail its production, distribution, and consumption, cocaine continues to be a significant global issue. The rise of the cocaine industry is rooted in a complex interplay of historical, economic, political, and social factors, and the challenges of tackling this problem persist in the present day.

THE ORIGINS OF COCAINE: FROM ANCIENT RITUALS TO MODERN-DAY DRUGS

The story of cocaine begins in the Andean region of South America, where indigenous peoples have cultivated the coca plant for thousands of years. The coca plant (Erythroxylum coca) has been used by Andean societies for medicinal, ceremonial, and recreational purposes. Its leaves contain alkaloids that, when chewed, provide stimulant effects. For the indigenous people, coca leaves were consumed to counteract the effects of high-altitude living, providing energy and reducing fatigue.

In its natural form, coca leaf does not produce the intense and addictive effects associated with refined cocaine. However, the process of isolating and refining the active ingredient, cocaine hydrochloride, has led to the creation of a potent and illegal drug.

THE DISCOVERY OF COCAINE AS A PSYCHOACTIVE SUBSTANCE

The active compound in coca, known as "cocaine," was first isolated in the mid-19th century by European chemists. In 1860, German chemist Albert Niemann isolated the alkaloid from coca leaves and named it "cocaine." During this period, cocaine became a popular substance in Europe and the United States for its stimulating properties. It was used in various products, including tonics, medicines, and even in beverages such as Coca-Cola, which initially contained coca extract.

Cocaine was widely used in the medical field in the late 19th and early 20th centuries, being promoted as a cure for various ailments, including depression, fatigue, and pain. However, it soon became evident that the drug had a high potential for abuse and addiction. By the early 20th century, authorities began regulating the drug, and its medical use was gradually phased out due to concerns over its harmful effects.

Despite the early efforts to control cocaine, the global demand for the drug continued to rise. The refinement of cocaine into its modern, potent form contributed to its widespread illegal use, particularly in the United States and Europe.

THE RISE OF THE COCAINE TRADE: FROM LOCAL SUPPLY TO GLOBAL DEMAND

While coca leaves were traditionally cultivated in the Andean region for centuries, the industrial-scale production of cocaine as an illicit commodity began in the 1950s and 1960s. During this period, cocaine trafficking networks began to emerge in Colombia, Peru, and Bolivia, with the primary goal of supplying demand in the United States and Europe.

In Colombia, the production of cocaine expanded rapidly in the 1970s. The nation's geographic location and proximity to key smuggling routes, coupled with the availability of coca crops, made it an ideal center for cocaine production. Colombian drug cartels, such as the infamous Medellín and Cali cartels, played a key role in the rapid rise of the cocaine trade. These cartels utilized sophisticated methods to process raw coca leaves into refined cocaine, which could then be smuggled into the United States and beyond.

The Medellín cartel, led by the notorious Pablo Escobar, became a dominant force in the cocaine trade during the 1980s. At its peak, the Medellín cartel controlled as much as 80% of the global cocaine supply, generating billions of dollars in profits annually. The cartel's influence was so pervasive that it infiltrated every level of Colombian society, including the government, law enforcement, and military. The cartel also used extreme violence to maintain control over the cocaine trade, leading to widespread corruption and instability.

The success of the Medellín cartel was followed by the rise of the Cali cartel, which was based in Colombia's capital, Cali. The Cali cartel, though less violent than the Medellín cartel, became a powerful player in the global cocaine market, further consolidating Colombia's role as the primary cocaine producer.

GLOBAL EXPANSION AND THE CREATION OF INTERNATIONAL NETWORKS

By the 1980s, cocaine had become one of the most lucrative illegal commodities in the world. The cocaine trade expanded beyond Colombia to involve other countries in South America, Central America, and the Caribbean. As Colombian cartels established smuggling routes to the United States and Europe, drug trafficking organizations from other countries became involved, including Mexico, which later became a major player in the trade.

Traffickers developed sophisticated smuggling methods, such as hiding cocaine in shipping containers, aircraft, and even the bodies of drug mules. The United States became the primary destination for cocaine, with demand for the drug peaking in the 1980s and 1990s. Cities like Miami and New York became key hubs for the distribution of cocaine, and the drug became a symbol of excess and hedonism in popular culture.

Despite the massive wealth generated by the cocaine trade, the consequences of the industry began to emerge. The violence associated with the drug trade, including turf wars between rival cartels, led to significant instability in Colombia and other countries in the region. In Colombia, the drug cartels used violence and intimidation to eliminate rivals, and assassinations of public officials, police officers, and journalists became commonplace.

U.S. GOVERNMENT RESPONSE: ANTI-DRUG CAMPAIGNS AND LAW ENFORCEMENT

In the 1980s and 1990s, the United States government declared a "War on Drugs," launching an aggressive campaign to reduce the production, trafficking, and consumption of cocaine and other illegal drugs. The U.S. government provided significant financial and logistical support to Latin American countries, particularly Colombia, to help combat the cocaine trade. This support included training and equipping local law enforcement and military forces to combat drug cartels, as well as providing financial assistance for anti-drug programs.

One of the most significant initiatives was the **Plan Colombia**, launched in 2000 with the goal of reducing cocaine production in Colombia. The plan involved a combination of military action, counter-narcotics operations, and social programs aimed at addressing the root causes of coca cultivation. Plan Colombia was heavily supported by the United States, which provided funding, equipment, and intelligence support to Colombian authorities.

The war on drugs also led to increased efforts to combat drug trafficking organizations operating in the United States. The U.S. Drug Enforcement Administration (DEA) conducted numerous operations aimed at dismantling drug cartels, and the FBI and local law enforcement agencies focused on disrupting drug distribution networks.

THE COLOMBIAN GOVERNMENT'S EFFORTS: THE DEMISE OF THE CARTELS

In response to the growing violence and instability caused by drug cartels, the Colombian government launched its own initiatives to combat the cocaine trade. The efforts to dismantle the Medellín and Cali cartels were particularly intense. The Colombian government, with the support of the United States, carried out targeted operations aimed at capturing or killing key cartel leaders.

The assassination of Pablo Escobar in 1993 was a significant turning point in the war against cocaine. Escobar's death weakened the Medellín cartel, but it did not end the cocaine trade. The Cali cartel was dismantled shortly thereafter, but new cartels, including the North Valley cartel and various paramilitary groups, emerged to take control of the cocaine trade.

Despite these successes, the Colombian government faced a persistent challenge in controlling coca cultivation and cocaine production. Efforts to eradicate coca crops through aerial spraying of herbicides and forced eradication programs led to widespread protests and criticism from local farmers, many of whom relied on coca cultivation for their livelihoods.

THE SHIFT IN COCAINE PRODUCTION: MEXICO AND BEYOND

While Colombia remains one of the world's largest producers of cocaine, Mexico has become an increasingly important player in the cocaine trade. Mexican drug trafficking organizations, such as the Sinaloa cartel, the Zetas, and the Jalisco New Generation cartel, have played a significant role in the trafficking of cocaine into the United States. These cartels have established smuggling routes that extend across Central America, utilizing Mexico as a key transit point for cocaine shipments.

In addition to Mexico, other countries in Latin America, such as Peru and Bolivia, continue to be significant producers of coca. Peru, in particular, has become one of the largest coca producers in the world, with many rural farmers growing coca as a cash crop due to its profitability compared to other agricultural products. Bolivia also remains a major coca-producing country, although the government of Evo Morales (who served as president from 2006 to 2019) implemented policies to reduce coca cultivation through a combination of alternative development programs and law enforcement measures.

Despite the concerted efforts to combat the cocaine trade, coca cultivation and cocaine production remain persistent problems. As long as there is demand for the drug, farmers and drug traffickers will continue to find ways to cultivate and produce cocaine.

THE ROLE OF GLOBAL DEMAND

The continued demand for cocaine in the United States, Europe, and other parts of the world is one of the primary drivers of the cocaine industry. Despite the efforts to reduce consumption through education campaigns and law enforcement initiatives, cocaine remains a widely used drug, particularly in urban areas and among high-income individuals.

The impact of cocaine addiction on public health and social stability is significant. Cocaine use has been linked to a range of physical and mental health issues, including heart disease, stroke, anxiety, and psychosis. The drug's high potential for addiction has contributed to an ongoing crisis in many communities, particularly in the United States and Europe, where cocaine use remains prevalent.

In addition to the health risks, cocaine trafficking contributes to violence and instability in producer and transit countries. The profits from the cocaine trade fund organized crime and violence, leading to a range of social and political problems. Corruption, lawlessness, and weak institutions are often exacerbated by the presence of the cocaine industry, making it difficult for governments to address the issue effectively.

INTERNATIONAL COOPERATION: THE ROLE OF THE UN AND REGIONAL EFFORTS

The United Nations Office on Drugs and Crime (UNODC) plays a critical role in coordinating international efforts to combat the cocaine trade. The UNODC works with countries around the world to provide technical assistance, policy advice, and support for drug control programs. The organization also works to strengthen international cooperation and build the capacity of law enforcement agencies to combat drug trafficking.

In addition to the UN's efforts, regional organizations such as the Organization of American States (OAS) and the Inter-American Drug Abuse Control Commission (CICAD) have worked to promote drug control strategies across the Americas. These organizations aim to reduce the demand for illicit drugs, strengthen law enforcement cooperation, and promote alternative development programs for coca farmers.

THE CHALLENGES OF ADDRESSING THE COCAINE TRADE

Despite the efforts of governments and international organizations, addressing the cocaine trade remains an incredibly complex and challenging task. Coca cultivation and cocaine production continue to thrive due to the high profitability of the industry, the demand for the drug, and the lack of alternatives for rural farmers in producer countries.

In Colombia, Peru, and Bolivia, the issue of coca cultivation is intertwined with poverty and limited access to economic opportunities. For many farmers, coca is the most lucrative crop available, making it difficult for them to transition to alternative forms of agriculture. Furthermore, the presence of powerful criminal organizations that control the cocaine trade makes it difficult for governments to implement effective solutions.

CONCLUSION: THE PERSISTENT CHALLENGE OF THE COCAINE INDUSTRY

The rise of the cocaine industry is a story of global demand, economic opportunity, and social consequences. From its ancient roots in the Andes to its status as a global illicit trade, cocaine remains one of the most pervasive and damaging drugs in the world. The cocaine trade generates billions of dollars annually, fueling violence, corruption, and instability across Latin America and beyond.

Efforts to combat the cocaine industry have been ongoing for decades, with governments, international organizations, and law enforcement agencies working to dismantle trafficking networks and reduce demand. However, the continued production of coca, the involvement of powerful criminal organizations, and the persistent demand for cocaine present ongoing challenges.

To effectively address the problem of the cocaine industry, a multi-faceted approach is required—one that combines law enforcement efforts with strategies for reducing demand, providing alternative livelihoods for farmers, and addressing the root causes of poverty and violence. Only through sustained, cooperative global efforts can the cocaine trade be significantly reduced and its damaging effects mitigated.

CHAPTER 20
THE BOSTON MARATHON BOMBING
COWARDLY ATTACK ON INNOCENT PEOPLE

Dzhokhar Tsarnaev

On April 15, 2013, two bombs exploded near the finish line of the Boston Marathon, killing three people and injuring over 260 others. The attack shocked the nation and the world, marking the most significant act of terrorism in the United States since 9/11. The Boston Marathon bombings were the work of two brothers, Tamerlan and Dzhokhar Tsarnaev, who carried out the attack as part of their jihadist-inspired plot. The bombing, its aftermath, and the subsequent manhunt became an international news story, revealing both the vulnerabilities and the resilience of a society confronted with terrorism.

BACKGROUND AND MOTIVATION THE TSARNAEV BROTHERS

Tamerlan Tsarnaev, born in 1986 in Kyrgyzstan, and his younger brother Dzhokhar Tsarnaev, born in 1993 in the former Soviet republic of Tajikistan, were ethnic Chechens who had moved to the United States with their family in 2002, seeking asylum from political unrest in Russia. They settled in Cambridge, Massachusetts, where they attended high school and, in Tamerlan's case, began studying engineering at Bunker Hill Community College.

Tamerlan Tsarnaev had a history of radicalizing views that emerged in the years leading up to the bombing. He was reportedly influenced by extremist Islamic ideologies, having attended a mosque in Boston that was linked to several radical figures. He became increasingly vocal about his beliefs, expressing disdain for Western values and even going so far as to justify violence against Americans. He also began spending time with people sympathetic to militant Islamist movements, including a former friend who was later revealed to have been involved in jihadist networks in the Middle East.

Dzhokhar Tsarnaev, by contrast, appeared to be more assimilated into American life. A promising student who had received a scholarship to attend the University of Massachusetts Dartmouth, he was not initially known for holding radical views. However, over time, Dzhokhar became increasingly influenced by his older brother's radicalization. Tamerlan reportedly pressured Dzhokhar to adopt a similar ideology, and it was through Tamerlan's influence that Dzhokhar became involved in the planning of the attack.

Both brothers were reportedly inspired by jihadist rhetoric, including the teachings of Al-Qaeda. The 2011 death of Osama bin Laden and the continued reports of jihadist activity in Syria, Iraq, and Afghanistan likely further fueled their resolve. They believed that carrying out an attack on U.S. soil would help them make a political and religious statement and retaliate against the perceived injustices faced by Muslims around the world.

RADICALIZATION AND MOTIVATION

The Tsarnaev brothers' motivation for the bombing was primarily driven by their extremist interpretation of Islam. The brothers were radicalized by online materials and speeches of influential figures, such as Anwar al-Awlaki, an American-born cleric and leader of Al-Qaeda in the Arabian Peninsula (AQAP). Al-Awlaki had become an influential figure in the world of jihadist ideologies, and his calls for violence against Americans resonated with the Tsarnaevs.

Tamerlan, particularly, began to see the United States as the primary enemy of Muslims worldwide, believing that it was a duty to strike at American interests and to carry out acts of violence against civilians as retribution for perceived injustices. The brothers' actions were motivated by a mix of personal grievances and the desire to achieve international recognition for their jihadist cause. Their decision to attack a major American public event, the Boston Marathon, was both symbolic and tactical. It was a high-profile target that would attract massive media coverage, thereby giving their attack global visibility.

PLANNING THE ATTACK

In the months leading up to the Boston Marathon bombing, the Tsarnaev brothers took several key steps in planning their attack. The brothers initially considered targeting other locations, but ultimately chose the Boston Marathon as their preferred site due to its high profile.

Tamerlan began purchasing the materials necessary for the bomb, including pressure cookers, which would be used to create the bomb's casing. The brothers also bought black powder, a key ingredient in the explosive devices they would construct. These materials were bought from various online retailers and local stores, and they were prepared in secret, often in Tamerlan's apartment.

Dzhokhar, who had become increasingly involved in his brother's activities, played a significant role in carrying out the logistics of the bombing. Although Dzhokhar initially seemed less committed to the jihadist cause, he eventually became an active participant, following Tamerlan's lead and learning how to make bombs and execute the attack.

Tamerlan, on the other hand, took the lead in planning the specifics of the bombing. He chose to use pressure cookers because they were inexpensive, readily available, and could be packed with explosive material. He had also watched bomb-making tutorials online, which guided him in constructing the devices. The choice of the Boston Marathon as a target was made for its public visibility, mass crowding, and symbolic importance.

SURVEILLANCE AND RECONNAISSANCE

In the weeks leading up to the attack, the Tsarnaev brothers conducted surveillance of the Boston Marathon route, identifying key locations near the finish line where the bombs could cause maximum casualties. They spent several days walking around the area and observing the crowds. The brothers noted the layout of the race, paying particular attention to the places where spectators would gather.

On the day of the attack, they arrived at the scene and placed their bombs in two separate locations, close to the finish line. Their goal was not just to kill but to instill fear by making the bombs as deadly and destructive as possible. They planned to detonate the devices remotely, with the use of timers designed to go off at specific intervals.

THE EXECUTION OF THE ATTACK

April 15, 2013, was the day of the Boston Marathon, a highly anticipated event that attracts runners and spectators from around the world. The race was being held on Patriots' Day, a public holiday in Massachusetts. The atmosphere was festive, with thousands of spectators lining the streets and cheering on the runners. It was a highly public event, providing an ideal stage for the Tsarnaev brothers' attack.

The brothers had constructed two pressure cooker bombs, each filled with explosives, nails, and ball bearings to maximize the devastation. The bombs were placed in backpacks and left on the ground near the finish line, where the largest crowds were gathered. The first bomb was placed near the intersection of Boylston Street and Exeter Street, and the second bomb was placed near the intersection of Boylston Street and Dartmouth Street.

At approximately 2:49 p.m., the first bomb detonated, causing an explosion that left three people dead and more than 170 injured. The bomb's blast was devastating, with shrapnel and debris flying in all directions. Just 12 seconds later, the second bomb exploded, causing even more casualties.

The explosions were chaotic and left the streets of Boston covered in debris and blood. The scene was filled with panic, confusion, and terror. The explosions caused widespread damage, including the destruction of storefronts, windows, and vehicles in the area.

THE AFTERMATH AND INVESTIGATION

In the immediate aftermath of the bombings, emergency responders and law enforcement officers rushed to the scene to assist the injured and secure the area. The Boston Police Department (BPD), Massachusetts State Police, and federal agencies such as the FBI quickly began the process of investigating the attack.

The chaos surrounding the bombings created significant challenges for first responders, but the rapid mobilization of law enforcement helped save lives. Hospitals around Boston were put on high alert, and trauma centers were prepared to treat victims of the bombing.

Within hours of the explosions, investigators began piecing together evidence. Security cameras from nearby businesses captured images of the Tsarnaev brothers, though they were not immediately identified. However, law enforcement agencies soon focused their attention on the brothers as suspects in the bombing.

THE MANHUNT

The investigation into the bombings quickly evolved into a nationwide manhunt. The FBI, in collaboration with local law enforcement and federal agencies, launched a public appeal for information and released photographs and video footage of the suspects. On April 18, 2013, the FBI identified Tamerlan and Dzhokhar Tsarnaev as the primary suspects in the bombing.

The discovery led to widespread media coverage, and within hours, the brothers were involved in a violent confrontation with police. On the night of April 18, the Tsarnaev brothers attempted to flee, leading to a shootout with police in the suburb of Watertown, Massachusetts. Tamerlan was killed in the exchange of gunfire, while Dzhokhar managed to escape on foot.

The manhunt for Dzhokhar Tsarnaev continued for several more days, as the authorities went door-to-door in search of the fugitive. On April 19, 2013, after an intense search and lockdown of the city, Dzhokhar Tsarnaev was captured in a boat in the backyard of a house in Watertown. He was taken into custody and later charged with multiple crimes, including the use of a weapon of mass destruction.

LEGAL PROCEEDINGS AND CONSEQUENCES

In the years following the attack, Dzhokhar Tsarnaev was put on trial for his role in the bombing. He was convicted on 30 counts, including murder, use of a weapon of mass destruction, and conspiracy to use a weapon of mass destruction. In 2015, he was sentenced to death for his crimes, though his sentence was later appealed and overturned by a federal appeals court in 2020.

The Boston Marathon bombings led to a national debate about security, surveillance, and counterterrorism. While the tragedy highlighted vulnerabilities in the U.S. security apparatus, it also demonstrated the resilience of the American public. The city of Boston rallied together in the aftermath of the attack, with many people participating in the "Boston Strong" movement to support the victims and their families.

CONCLUSION

The Boston Marathon bombings were a horrifying act of terrorism that shocked the United States and the world. The planning and execution of the attack were marked by careful preparation and the brothers' desire to make a bold statement against American values. While Tamerlan and Dzhokhar Tsarnaev's motivations were rooted in extremist ideology, their actions also reflected broader global trends of terrorism and violence.

In the years following the attack, the bombing prompted an outpouring of support for the victims and led to important discussions about counterterrorism policies and security. The Boston Marathon bombing was a tragic reminder of the potential for violence in the modern world and the need for continued vigilance in the fight against terrorism.

CHAPTER 21
THE MOSCOW THEATER HOSTAGE CRISIS
BAD SITUATION WORSENED BY BAD DECISIONS

Russian Special Forces Storm The Theater

The Moscow Theater Siege, also known as the 2002 Dubrovka Theater Hostage Crisis, was one of the most harrowing and complex hostage situations in modern Russian history. It unfolded in the heart of Moscow, involving a group of Chechen militants, a theater full of innocent civilians, and Russian security forces. Over a three-day period, this event captured global attention, and its aftermath would leave deep marks on Russian society, politics, and its approach to counterterrorism.

ORIGINS OF THE MOSCOW THEATER SIEGE

The roots of the Moscow theater siege lie within the complex, violent history of the Chechen-Russian conflict. The Chechen struggle for independence from Russia had been ongoing for centuries, but the modern phase of the conflict began in the early 1990s following the collapse of the Soviet Union. After declaring independence in 1991, Chechnya was drawn into a brutal war with Russia. The First Chechen War (1994-1996) ended with Chechnya gaining de facto independence, but the cost of the war was devastating. The loss of life was enormous, and much of the region's infrastructure was destroyed.

However, in 1999, a second war broke out following a series of apartment bombings in Russia, which the Russian government blamed on Chechen militants. This led to the Russian military re-entering Chechnya. Over the next few years, the region was characterized by insurgency and ongoing violence as the Russian state sought to suppress Chechen independence movements.

During this period, a group of radical Chechen separatists, led by figures like Shamil Basayev and others aligned with him, began to adopt increasingly violent and internationalist tactics. The rise of Islamic fundamentalism, both within Chechnya and in the broader North Caucasus, contributed to an atmosphere of extremism. The hostage-taking at the Dubrovka Theater would be a direct expression of this radicalization.

THE CONTEXT: CHECHEN EXTREMISTS AND THE MOSCOW THEATER

By 2002, the Russian government had largely regained control over Chechnya, but the region remained unstable. Chechen separatists were not entirely defeated, and guerrilla warfare continued in the mountainous regions. The population in Chechnya suffered immensely under the heavy-handed tactics of the Russian military, with widespread human rights abuses reported on both sides.

In this context, some Chechen militants turned to terrorist tactics, including taking hostages in order to draw attention to their cause. In 2002, a group of Chechen militants, under the leadership of a man named Movsar Barayev, planned and executed the Moscow Theater Siege.

The Dubrovka Theater, located in the southern part of Moscow, was chosen as the site for this audacious attack. The theater, which could hold over 1,000 people, was hosting a popular musical production, *Nord-Ost*, at the time. The choice of this venue was significant — it was a symbol of cultural life in Moscow, and its patrons were seen as representing the Russian elite and middle class. This made it an ideal target for the Chechen militants, who sought to make a dramatic statement.

The hostages were seized on 23 October during Act II of a sold-out performance of *Nord-Ost* a little after 9:00 PM, 40–50 heavily armed masked men and women drove in a bus to the theater and entered the main hall firing assault rifles in the air.[10]

The black-and-camouflage-clad attackers[11] took approximately 850–900 people hostage, including members of the audience and performers, among them an MVD general. The reaction of spectators inside the theater to the news that the theater was under terrorist attack was not uniform: some people remained calm, some reacted hysterically, and others fainted. Some performers who had been resting backstage escaped through an open window and called the police; in all, some 90 people managed to flee the building or hide.

The militants were well-armed and prepared for a prolonged standoff. They had explosives, automatic weapons, and a well-organized plan to keep the hostages under control. Their primary goal was to draw attention to the ongoing conflict in Chechnya and force the Russian government to negotiate. The militants were led by Barayev, who had previously been involved in other terrorist acts.

THE RUSSIAN RESPONSE

The Russian government, led by President Vladimir Putin, quickly responded to the theater siege. Putin had been in power since 1999, and his administration was characterized by a strong emphasis on state security, a crackdown on separatism, and an uncompromising stance toward Chechnya. The Russian authorities were determined not to negotiate with terrorists, a policy that had been set during the earlier stages of the Chechen conflict. Despite this stance, there was enormous pressure to resolve the crisis peacefully, as the lives of the hostages were at stake.

The Russian government began by surrounding the theater with security forces, including the FSB (Federal Security Service) and the special forces unit, Alpha Group. The hostage-takers were in communication with the authorities, but their demands remained unchanged: a withdrawal of Russian forces from Chechnya. As the hours passed, it became increasingly clear that the militants were not going to surrender or negotiate, and the authorities began to prepare for a more forceful resolution to the crisis.

The Russian government also faced significant public pressure to resolve the situation quickly, as news of the siege spread across the world. The international community was watching closely, and many governments, including the United States and European countries, expressed their concerns and urged the Russian authorities to find a peaceful resolution.

Despite the tension, the situation continued for several days, with periodic exchanges of gunfire between the militants and Russian forces. During this time, some hostages were released, and others were allowed to make contact with their families. The militants made several threats to kill hostages if their demands were not met, and they also stated that they would detonate explosives inside the theater if the Russian military attempted to storm the building.

THE USE OF GAS: A CONTROVERSIAL DECISION

On the third day of the siege, the Russian authorities made a controversial decision. In an attempt to resolve the situation without a full-scale assault, they decided to use a chemical agent, later identified as a form of fentanyl, to incapacitate the hostage-takers. The gas was pumped into the theater's ventilation system, hoping to render the militants unconscious or incapacitated without killing the hostages.

The use of the gas was a highly risky and unprecedented measure. While the intent was to neutralize the hostage-takers without killing the civilians, there were significant consequences. The gas quickly spread throughout the theater, and within hours, all of the militants were incapacitated. However, the gas also had unintended and lethal effects on the hostages. Many of them began to show signs of poisoning, including difficulty breathing, confusion, and unconsciousness.

At the same time, the Russian authorities prepared for an assault. Alpha Group stormed the building, and in a matter of minutes, they killed all the militants. However, the gas had already caused widespread harm. When the security forces entered the theater, they found many hostages in critical condition, and by the time they were evacuated, over 100 hostages had died from the effects of the gas.

The Aftermath

In total, 170 people died as a result of the Moscow Theater Siege, including 130 hostages and all 40 of the militants. The gas used by Russian forces was confirmed as a derivative of fentanyl. The exact formulation and dosage used remain a subject of debate, as many of the hostages who survived suffered from severe health complications due to the gas.

The siege had profound consequences for Russia, both domestically and internationally. The Russian government was criticized for its handling of the situation, particularly for the use of gas without informing the hostages or their families of the potential dangers. The decision to storm the building and the subsequent deaths raised questions about the effectiveness of Russian counterterrorism tactics, as well as the ethics of using chemical agents in such situations.

For the families of the victims, the aftermath was marked by grief, anger, and a sense of betrayal. Many felt that the Russian government had sacrificed the lives of innocent civilians in the pursuit of political goals. Some survivors faced long-term health problems as a result of the gas exposure, and many continued to suffer from psychological trauma.

The siege also had broader implications for Russia's approach to counterterrorism. It highlighted the need for a more nuanced strategy, balancing force with negotiation and minimizing civilian casualties. The event underscored the ongoing instability in Chechnya and the broader North Caucasus, where terrorism and insurgency remained potent threats.

On the international stage, the Moscow Theater Siege became a symbol of the dangers of radicalism, both in Chechnya and globally. It drew attention to the plight of civilians caught in the crossfire of larger geopolitical conflicts, as well as the role of terrorism in shaping global security policies. The siege was also a reminder of the challenges of dealing with hostage situations in an increasingly complex and dangerous world.

CONCLUSION

The Moscow Theater Siege was a tragic event that marked a dark chapter in Russia's history. It was the culmination of years of violence in Chechnya and a reflection of the growing radicalization of some Chechen militants. The Russian government's decision to use a chemical agent to incapacitate the hostage-takers was controversial and ultimately led to the deaths of many innocent civilians. The aftermath of the siege prompted widespread reflection on the effectiveness of counterterrorism strategies, the ethics of using chemical agents, and the human cost of political conflicts.

The siege also highlighted the need for a more balanced approach to counterterrorism, one that prioritizes the safety and well-being of civilians. In the years following the event, Russia continued to struggle with the complex dynamics of the Chechen conflict, as well as the broader challenge of dealing with terrorism and extremism. The legacy of the Moscow Theater Siege remains a painful reminder of the human toll of war, political strife, and violence.

CHAPTER 22
THE SEX GROOMING GANGS IN THE UK
A NATIONAL DISGRACE

24 Convicted Sex Criminals

The issue of grooming gangs in the United Kingdom has become one of the most contentious and distressing social problems in recent years. The term "grooming gangs" refers to groups of men, often from specific ethnic communities, who exploit vulnerable young people for sexual purposes. These gangs typically target girls from disadvantaged backgrounds, subjecting them to manipulation, coercion, and abuse. The scale of the problem, its impact on victims, and the often sensitive nature of the perpetrators' identities have sparked heated debates about race, religion, social class, and the role of authorities in preventing and prosecuting such crimes. This account seeks to provide a comprehensive analysis of the issue, tracing its origins, impact, and responses from society, law enforcement, and government.

ORIGINS AND THE EMERGENCE OF THE ISSUE

The problem of grooming gangs in the UK began to emerge into public consciousness in the early 2000s, although cases of sexual exploitation had likely been occurring for decades prior. The phenomenon was initially brought to light through investigative journalism and court cases, particularly in cities such as Rotherham, Rochdale, and Oxford. These areas became synonymous with the issue of grooming gangs due to the high-profile prosecutions that brought attention to the scale of the problem.

Historically, child sexual exploitation in the UK was not seen as a distinct social issue but rather as part of broader concerns about child abuse. However, by the early 21st century, a pattern began to emerge, where certain ethnic communities were being disproportionately linked to grooming activities. In particular, men of Pakistani and Bangladeshi descent were frequently implicated, leading to accusations of a specific cultural and religious basis for the abuse. The term "grooming gangs" was coined to describe organized groups of perpetrators who exploited young girls, often by offering them gifts, alcohol, and drugs, in exchange for sexual favours.

These cases often involved multiple perpetrators over extended periods. Victims were typically girls from disadvantaged backgrounds, including those in care homes, with poor family relationships, or those who were otherwise vulnerable. The abuse was systematic and involved a number of perpetrators, sometimes running into the dozens. In many cases, the victims were trafficked between cities and towns, sometimes crossing multiple counties, to be exploited by different men in different locations.

THE SCOPE OF THE PROBLEM

The scale of the issue became evident in several high-profile cases, which highlighted the disturbing nature of grooming gangs across the UK. One of the most notorious cases occurred in Rotherham, South Yorkshire, where a report published by Professor Alexis Jay in 2014 revealed that over 1,400 children had been sexually exploited between 1997 and 2013. These children, mostly girls aged between 11 and 15, were systematically groomed and abused by men of South Asian descent. The grooming involved offering the girls alcohol, drugs, and attention, before coercing or forcing them into sex with multiple men.

The Rotherham case was followed by similar cases in other towns and cities, such as Rochdale, Oxford, and Telford. In Rochdale, a grooming gang was convicted in 2012 for exploiting young girls, some of whom were as young as 13. The perpetrators were predominantly of Pakistani heritage. Similarly, in Oxford, a grooming gang was convicted in 2013 for the exploitation of girls aged 11 to 15. The perpetrators in this case were also primarily men of Pakistani descent.

The number of such cases has led to growing concerns about the prevalence of grooming gangs in the UK. While there are no official statistics on the exact number of grooming gangs operating across the country, estimates suggest that there are several hundred known cases, affecting thousands of vulnerable young people. The problem is not limited to any one region, although certain areas, such as northern England, have seen a higher concentration of cases. Moreover, the issue has spread to towns and cities across the country, from the West Midlands to Yorkshire to the southeast.

The issue of grooming gangs has been particularly prevalent in some areas of West Yorkshire, where multiple high-profile cases of child sexual exploitation have taken place. One of the most significant of these cases involved the grooming and abuse of young girls by a group of men in towns such as Huddersfield, Bradford, and Leeds. These cases have garnered national attention due to the scale of the abuse, the involvement of organized criminal networks, and the perceived failure of authorities to act promptly or effectively in preventing the exploitation. Below, we delve into some of the most notable cases in West Yorkshire in detail.

THE HUDDERSFIELD CASE (2015–2018)

In 2015, a major child sexual exploitation (CSE) case emerged in Huddersfield, a town in West Yorkshire. This case involved a group of men who systematically groomed, abused, and exploited vulnerable young girls, some as young as 13. The victims, primarily white girls, were manipulated and coerced into sex by a group of men, who often provided alcohol, drugs, and promises of attention in exchange for sexual favours.

THE INVESTIGATION

The investigation into the abuse in Huddersfield began in earnest in 2015, when one of the victims came forward and reported the sexual exploitation. Following the report, West Yorkshire Police launched a large-scale investigation known as "Operation Tendersea." The investigation uncovered a network of men involved in grooming and exploiting young girls in Huddersfield, some of whom had been trafficked from other areas in Yorkshire.

A total of 20 men were eventually arrested and charged with various offenses, including rape, sexual assault, and trafficking. Many of the men were from Pakistani and Bangladeshi backgrounds, a factor that would later become a controversial aspect of the case. The investigation revealed that the men had used the same grooming techniques that had been seen in other areas of the UK, such as offering the girls gifts, alcohol, and drugs to gain their trust before coercing them into sexual activity.

The victims were often targeted because they were from vulnerable backgrounds, including girls from broken homes or those living in care. They were lured into relationships with older men who presented themselves as their protectors, only to later exploit them for sexual purposes. Many of the victims were frightened to speak out, fearing that their abusers would harm them or their families.

THE COURT CASE AND SENTENCING

In 2018, after a lengthy trial, a group of 20 men was convicted for their roles in the grooming and abuse of these young girls. The sentences ranged from several years in prison to life sentences for the most serious offenders. Some of the perpetrators were found guilty of multiple charges, with some having abused dozens of girls over an extended period.

The case drew widespread media attention due to the nature of the crimes and the fact that many of the perpetrators were from ethnic minority backgrounds, particularly Pakistani men. The trial was seen as another instance of grooming gangs targeting vulnerable young girls, often from white working-class backgrounds, in several northern English towns and cities. It was also part of a broader pattern of grooming and sexual exploitation that had been seen in cities like Rotherham, Rochdale, and Oxford.

BRADFORD (2010–2015)

Bradford, another city in West Yorkshire, has also been at the centre of high-profile grooming gang investigations. The city became the subject of scrutiny in 2010, when police uncovered a large-scale operation involving the sexual exploitation of young girls. The perpetrators, again predominantly from Pakistani heritage, were found to have groomed and abused a significant number of young victims over a period of several years.

THE INVESTIGATION

Bradford's child sexual exploitation scandal came to light in 2010, when a young girl came forward to report that she had been sexually assaulted by a group of men. This led to the formation of a police operation known as "Operation Newby," which aimed to investigate reports of sexual exploitation in the area. As the investigation progressed, officers discovered that numerous young girls had been coerced into sex by groups of men operating across the city. These men often frequented local takeaways, restaurants, and taxi ranks, where they would meet the vulnerable girls and lure them into sexual relationships.

The perpetrators used a variety of tactics to groom the victims, including providing them with gifts, alcohol, and drugs, and offering them attention and affection. Once the girls were under their control, the men would take advantage of them, often forcing them into sex and subjecting them to repeated abuse. Some of the girls were trafficked to other cities to be exploited further.

THE COURT CASE AND SENTENCING

In 2015, after an extensive investigation, a number of men were arrested and charged with offenses related to sexual exploitation and trafficking. The trial saw several individuals convicted for their roles in the abuse. A number of perpetrators were given long prison sentences, with some receiving life sentences for their involvement in the systematic exploitation of young girls. The sentencing was hailed as a major step forward in tackling the problem of grooming gangs in Bradford, though critics pointed out that the issue had been allowed to persist for far too long.

In the aftermath of the case, it became clear that there were significant failures within local authorities and law enforcement in Bradford to address the problem of child sexual exploitation. There were reports of victims being ignored or dismissed by social workers, and the police were accused of not taking the complaints of the victims seriously enough. As with other grooming gang cases in the UK, there were allegations that police were hesitant to investigate the perpetrators due to concerns about racial tensions and political correctness.

LEEDS (2007–2013)

Leeds, a major city in West Yorkshire, has also experienced its own share of child sexual exploitation cases involving grooming gangs. While the situation in Leeds did not receive as much media attention as cases in other areas like Rotherham or Rochdale, it still represented a disturbing pattern of abuse.

THE INVESTIGATION

The Leeds grooming case began to surface in the early 2000s, though it wasn't until later that the extent of the abuse was fully revealed. Several young girls came forward to report being sexually exploited by groups of men who had groomed them over an extended period. Once again the perpetrators were mostly of Pakistani and Bangladeshi descent, and again they often preyed on girls from vulnerable backgrounds, particularly those living in care homes or from troubled family situations.

Much like other cases, the grooming involved offering the girls gifts, alcohol, and drugs, in order to build trust and control. Once the perpetrators had gained the girls' trust, they would coerce them into sex, sometimes involving multiple men in a single instance. Some of the victims were trafficked to other towns and cities to be exploited further.

THE COURT CASE AND SENTENCING

Several men were arrested and convicted in connection with the abuse in Leeds. In 2013, a major trial led to the conviction of a group of men involved in grooming and abusing young girls in the city. The court heard how the perpetrators had sexually exploited multiple girls over several years, and some of the convicted men received significant prison sentences for their crimes.

As with other cases of grooming gangs, the prosecution of those responsible was seen as a step forward in holding perpetrators to account. However, there were still concerns about the failure of authorities to act sooner in Leeds. The city had witnessed multiple reports of child sexual exploitation, yet victims were not always taken seriously, and law enforcement was criticized for not adequately investigating the abuse when it was first reported.

THE GENDER AND ETHNIC DIMENSION

The issue of grooming gangs has been further complicated by the gender and ethnic makeup of the perpetrators. While the victims of grooming gangs are overwhelmingly female, the perpetrators are often men from specific ethnic backgrounds. This has raised difficult questions about the role of race, culture, and religion in the problem of child sexual exploitation.

In many of the cases that have come to public attention, the perpetrators have been described as being of Pakistani, Bangladeshi, or Afghan heritage. This has led to accusations of "Asian grooming gangs," which has sparked considerable debate. Critics argue that this term is overly broad and unfairly stigmatizes entire ethnic communities. They suggest that the issue is not so much about ethnicity or religion, but rather about a subculture of men within certain communities who view young girls as sexual prey.

On the other hand, some argue that cultural factors, such as the treatment of women within certain communities, play a role in grooming activities. Some experts have suggested that in conservative, patriarchal societies, women may be seen as objects to be controlled, which can contribute to a mindset that devalues young girls. Others point to the role of Islamic extremism in certain cases, though this remains a highly contentious point, with many rejecting the idea that religion is a driving factor in child sexual exploitation.

One of the key challenges is that the perpetrators often prey on vulnerable girls who are from working-class, white British backgrounds. Some critics argue that this aspect of the problem reflects deep-seated issues of racism, classism, and marginalization within British society. They suggest that authorities have been reluctant to act against grooming gangs for fear of being accused of racism, or because they viewed the girls as less valuable than other members of society. This reluctance, combined with a failure to act on early warnings, has led to a prolonged period during which grooming gangs were allowed to operate with impunity.

THE ROLE OF AUTHORITIES AND LAW ENFORCEMENT

One of the most disturbing aspects of the grooming gang issue is the failure of authorities to act promptly and effectively. In several high-profile cases, police, social workers, and local government officials were aware of the abuse but failed to take adequate steps to stop it. In the case of Rotherham, for example, police were reportedly aware of the abuse but were reluctant to intervene, partly because of concerns about racial tensions. In some instances, police officers allegedly failed to investigate cases of sexual exploitation because they feared being accused of racism or stirring up community unrest.

The failure to act was also compounded by a lack of understanding of grooming as a distinct form of sexual abuse. Traditionally, child sexual exploitation was thought to be an isolated issue, often involving one abuser and one victim. However, grooming gangs operate in a completely different way, involving multiple perpetrators and often targeting victims over long periods. This made it harder for authorities to identify the problem and respond appropriately.

In many cases, victims themselves were not believed or were dismissed as "delinquents" or "troublemakers." The girls, often from troubled or broken homes, were not taken seriously by social services or law enforcement, which led to their exploitation continuing unchecked. In some instances, victims were threatened or intimidated into silence, and in others, their reports were ignored by authorities who failed to understand the complex dynamics of grooming and exploitation.

The failure to take appropriate action led to widespread criticism of both local authorities and the police. In Rotherham, for instance, the 2014 report revealed that more than 1,400 children had been exploited, but the local authorities had failed to take decisive action, despite being aware of the problem for many years. The report stated that local authorities had prioritized political correctness over protecting vulnerable children, creating an environment in which grooming gangs could operate with relative ease.

Following the release of the report, there were calls for greater accountability among local authorities and law enforcement agencies. Many victims of grooming gangs, along with their supporters, accused the authorities of being complicit in the abuse by failing to act sooner. The report led to several resignations among local officials and police officers, and in some cases, criminal investigations were launched to examine how authorities had handled the situation.

LEGAL AND POLITICAL RESPONSES

In response to the grooming gang issue, the UK government has taken a number of legal and political steps to address the problem. In recent years, there has been an increased focus on improving the reporting and investigation of child sexual exploitation. The government has also implemented new legislation aimed at tackling child sexual abuse, including the Sexual Offences Act 2003, which created new categories of child sexual exploitation, and the Children and Families Act 2014, which introduced stronger measures for protecting children from abuse.

In addition to legal reforms, the government has also put pressure on local authorities and law enforcement agencies to improve their responses to grooming gangs. In 2016, the Home Office launched a national inquiry into child sexual abuse, which examined how institutions such as local authorities, the police, and social services had failed to protect vulnerable children from sexual exploitation. The inquiry sought to understand the scale of the problem and make recommendations for how authorities could better tackle grooming gangs.

Despite these efforts, many have argued that more needs to be done. Some have called for a stronger focus on preventing grooming and sexual exploitation through education and early intervention, particularly in communities where grooming gangs are most prevalent. Others have suggested that greater resources need to be allocated to law enforcement agencies to enable them to investigate grooming gangs more effectively and bring perpetrators to justice.

THE IMPACT ON VICTIMS

The impact of grooming gangs on their victims is profound and long-lasting. The psychological and emotional trauma inflicted on the young people involved in these crimes can be devastating. Many victims experience feelings of shame, guilt, and confusion, and may struggle with mental health issues such as depression, anxiety, and post-traumatic stress disorder (PTSD). The sense of betrayal that victims feel, both from the perpetrators and from the authorities who failed to protect them, can also lead to a loss of trust in institutions.

The exploitation often leaves victims with a distorted view of relationships, sex, and consent. They may struggle with forming healthy relationships later in life, and many victims require long-term therapy and support to overcome the trauma they experienced. Furthermore, the stigma attached to being a victim of grooming and sexual exploitation can cause social isolation and further marginalization, making it harder for victims to rebuild their lives.

CONCLUSION

The problem of grooming gangs in the UK is one of the most serious and disturbing forms of child sexual exploitation. It has exposed deep failures in the way authorities and society respond to sexual abuse and exploitation, particularly in relation to vulnerable young people. While significant progress has been made in raising awareness of the issue and improving legal frameworks, much remains to be done to ensure that victims are protected, perpetrators are held accountable, and grooming gangs are dismantled.

To truly tackle this issue, there needs to be a more comprehensive, coordinated approach that includes prevention, better support for victims, stronger law enforcement, and a commitment to addressing the root causes of exploitation. Only then can the UK begin to confront this dark chapter of its recent history and ensure that future generations of young people are better protected from sexual abuse and exploitation.

CHAPTER 23
THE MY LAI MASSACRE
FUELED BY HATE AND FRUSTRATION

Women & Children Before The Massacre

The My Lai Massacre, one of the darkest chapters of the Vietnam War, remains a powerful and painful symbol of the horrors of war and the moral and ethical dilemmas faced by soldiers. It is a haunting example of the brutalization of human beings in a conflict, the erosion of morality under the pressures of war, and the long-lasting impact that such events have on both the victims and those who carry out such acts.

This chapter will provide a comprehensive account of the My Lai Massacre, including the events leading up to the massacre, the events themselves, the aftermath, and the wider impact it had on American society and military culture. It will also explore the political and ethical dimensions of the massacre and its legacy.

CONTEXT OF THE VIETNAM WAR AND THE MY LAI MASSACRE

The Vietnam War was a complex and highly controversial conflict that spanned from the mid-1950s to 1975. It was primarily a struggle between communist North Vietnam, led by Ho Chi Minh, and the South Vietnamese government, which was supported by the United States and other anti-communist allies. The United States became heavily involved in the conflict in the early 1960s, first through military advisors and later through large-scale military intervention. The U.S. involvement in Vietnam was part of a broader strategy to contain the spread of communism, often referred to as the "Domino Theory," which held that if one country in Southeast Asia fell to communism, others would follow suit.

The war became increasingly brutal as it dragged on, with both sides committing acts of violence against civilians. The U.S. military's tactics in Vietnam included widespread airstrikes, the use of chemical defoliants like Agent Orange, and counterinsurgency operations aimed at eradicating the Viet Cong and North Vietnamese forces. The conflict led to the deaths of millions of Vietnamese civilians and soldiers, as well as tens of thousands of American soldiers.

One of the key aspects of the war was the difficulty in distinguishing between combatants and civilians, especially in rural areas where the Viet Cong were often embedded in the local population. The war was also marked by deepening divisions within American society, with widespread protests and anti-war sentiment growing as the war dragged on.

It was in this brutal and dehumanizing context that the My Lai Massacre took place.

THE PRELUDE TO MY LAI: OPERATION WHEELER AND THE SEARCH FOR THE VIET CONG

The massacre occurred on March 16, 1968, in the hamlets of My Lai and My Khe, located in Quang Ngai Province in South Vietnam. These villages were believed to be strongholds of the Viet Cong, the communist guerrilla fighters who were fighting against the South Vietnamese government and the U.S. military.

At the time, the U.S. military had launched a series of operations aimed at rooting out the Viet Cong from rural areas in Vietnam. One such operation was called "Operation Wheeler," a large-scale search-and-destroy mission that took place in the My Lai area. The purpose of the operation was to eliminate the Viet Cong fighters who were believed to be hiding in the villages, as well as to gather intelligence about their activities. The U.S. military was under tremendous pressure to deliver quick results and demonstrate progress in the war effort, and this led to an increasingly aggressive and indiscriminate approach to warfare.

The military strategy during this period often led to mass civilian casualties. Villages were routinely destroyed, and civilians were often treated as potential insurgents. The line between combatants and non-combatants was blurred, and this set the stage for what would unfold in My Lai.

THE MASSACRE: MARCH 16, 1968

On the morning of 16 March at 07:30, around 100 soldiers from Charlie Company led by Medina, following a short artillery and helicopter gunship barrage, landed in helicopters at Sơn Mỹ, a patchwork of individual homesteads, grouped settlements, rice paddies, irrigation ditches, dikes, and dirt roads, connecting an assortment of hamlets and sub-hamlets. The largest among them were the hamlets Mỹ Lai, Cổ Lũy, Mỹ Khê, and Tu Cung.

The GIs expected to engage the Vietcong Local Force 48th Battalion, which was one of the Vietcong's most successful units. Although the GIs were not fired upon after landing, they still suspected there were VC guerrillas hiding underground or in the huts. Confirming their suspicions, the gunships engaged several armed enemies in the vicinity of Mỹ Lai, killing four; later, one weapon was retrieved from the site.

According to the operational plan, 1st Platoon, led by Second Lieutenant (2LT) William Calley and 2nd Platoon, led by 2LT Stephen Brooks, entered the hamlet of Tu Cung in line formation at 08:00, while the 3rd Platoon, commanded by 2LT Jeffrey U. Lacross, and Captain Medina's command post remained outside. On approach, both platoons fired at people they saw in the rice fields and in the brush.

Instead of the expected enemy, the GIs found women, children and old men, many of whom were cooking breakfast over outdoor fires. The villagers were getting ready for a market day and at first did not panic or run away as they were herded into the hamlet's common spaces and homestead yards. Harry Stanley, a machine gunner from Charlie Company, said during the U.S Army Criminal Investigation Division inquiry that the killings started without warning. He first observed a member of 1st Platoon strike a Vietnamese man with a bayonet. Then the same trooper pushed another villager into a well and threw a grenade in the well. Next, he saw fifteen or twenty people, mainly women and children, kneeling around a temple with burning incense. They were praying and crying. They were all killed by shots to the head.

Most of the killings occurred in the southern part of Tu Cung, a sub-hamlet of Xom Lang, which was a home to 700 residents. Xom Lang was erroneously marked on the U.S. military operational maps of Quảng Ngãi Province as Mỹ Lai.

A large group of approximately 70–80 villagers was rounded up by 1st Platoon in Xom Lang and led to an irrigation ditch east of the settlement. They were then pushed into the ditch and shot dead by soldiers after repeated orders issued by Calley, who was also shooting. PFC Paul Meadlo testified that he expended several M16 rifle magazines. He recollected that women were saying "No VC" and were trying to shield their children. He remembered that he was shooting old men and women, ranging in ages from grandmothers to teenagers, many with babies or small children in their arms, since he was convinced at that time that they were all booby-trapped with grenades and poised to attack. On another occasion during the security sweep of My Lai, Meadlo again fired into civilians side by side with Lieutenant Calley.

PFC Dennis Konti, a witness for the prosecution, told of one especially gruesome episode during the shooting, "A lot of women had thrown themselves on top of the children to protect them, and the children were alive at first. Then, the children who were old enough to walk got up and Calley began to shoot the children". Other 1st Platoon members testified that many of the deaths of individual Vietnamese men, women and children occurred inside Mỹ Lai during the security sweep. To ensure the hamlets could no longer offer support to the enemy, the livestock was shot as well.

When PFC Michael Bernhardt entered the subhamlet of Xom Lang, the massacre was underway:

I walked up and saw these guys doing strange things. Setting fire to the hootches and huts and waiting for people to come out and then shooting them... going into the hootches and shooting them up ... gathering people in groups and shooting them... As I walked in you could see piles of people all through the village. all over. They were gathered up into large groups. I saw them shoot an M79 grenade launcher into a group of people who were still alive. But it was mostly done with a machine gun. They were shooting women and children just like anybody else. We met no resistance and I only saw three captured weapons. We had no casualties. It was just like any other Vietnamese village – old papa-sans, women and kids. As a matter of fact, I don't remember seeing one military-age male in the entire place, dead or alive.

One group of 20–50 villagers was herded south of Xom Lang and killed on a dirt road. According to U.S. Army photographer Sgt. Ronald Haeberle's eyewitness account of the massacre, in one instance,

There were some South Vietnamese people, maybe fifteen of them, women and children included, walking on a dirt road maybe 100 yards [90 m] away. All of a sudden the GIs just opened up with M16s. Beside the M16 fire, they were shooting at the people with M79 grenade launchers ... I couldn't believe what I was seeing.

Calley testified that he heard the shooting and arrived on the scene. He observed his men firing into a ditch with Vietnamese people inside, then began to take part in the shooting himself, using an M16 from a distance of no more than 5 feet (1.5m). During the massacre, a helicopter landed on the other side of the ditch and the pilot asked Calley if they could provide any medical assistance to the wounded civilians in Mỹ Lai; Calley admitted replying that "a hand grenade was the only available means he had for their evacuation". At 11:00 Medina radioed an order to cease fire, and 1st Platoon took a break, during which they ate lunch.

An unidentified man and child who were killed on a road

Members of 2nd Platoon killed at least 60–70 Vietnamese, as they swept through the northern half of Mỹ Lai and through Binh Tay, a small sub-hamlet about 400 metres (1,300 ft) north of Mỹ Lai. After the initial sweeps by 1st and 2nd Platoons, 3rd Platoon was dispatched to deal with any "remaining resistance". 3rd Platoon, which stayed in reserve, reportedly rounded up and killed a group of seven to twelve women and children.

Since Charlie Company had not met any enemy opposition at Mỹ Lai and did not request back-up, Bravo Company, 4th Battalion, 3rd Infantry Regiment of TF Barker was transported by air between 08:15 and 08:30 3 km (2180 km mi) away. It attacked the subhamlet My Hoi of the hamlet known as Cô Lũy, which was mapped by the Army as Mỹ Khê. During this operation, between 60 and 155 people, including women and children, were killed.

Over the remaining day, both companies were involved in the further burning and destruction of dwellings, as well as continued mistreatment of Vietnamese detainees. While it was noted in the Courts Martial proceedings that some soldiers of Charlie Company did not participate in any killings, it was noted they neither openly protested against them nor filed complaints later to their superiors.

William Thomas Allison, a professor of Military History at Georgia Southern University, wrote, "By midmorning, members of Charlie Company had killed hundreds of civilians and raped or assaulted countless women and young girls. They encountered no enemy fire and found no weapons in My Lai itself".

By the time the killings stopped, Charlie Company had suffered one casualty– a soldier who had intentionally shot himself in the foot to avoid participating in the massacre– and just three enemy weapons were confiscated.

THE COVER-UP AND DISCOVERY

In the immediate aftermath of the massacre, the U.S. Army attempted to cover up the events that had transpired in My Lai. Lieutenant Calley, the officer in charge of Charlie Company, and other officers who had been involved in the massacre were not initially held accountable. Instead, the military reported the operation as a success, claiming that they had eliminated a significant number of Viet Cong fighters in the area.

However, evidence of the massacre began to emerge over the next year. The cover-up was exposed in part thanks to the efforts of a whistleblower, Warrant Officer Hugh Thompson. Thompson, a helicopter pilot who had been flying in the area during the operation, became aware of the killings and attempted to intervene. He landed his helicopter between the soldiers and the remaining villagers and ordered the soldiers to stop the violence.

Thompson also reported the massacre to his superiors, but his warnings were initially ignored.

The truth about My Lai began to surface when investigative journalist Seymour Hersh broke the story in November 1969. Hersh's reporting, which included interviews with soldiers who had witnessed the massacre and with survivors, brought the events at My Lai to public attention. The U.S. Army launched an official investigation into the massacre, and in 1971, Lieutenant Calley was put on trial for murder.

THE TRIAL AND AFTERMATH

The trial of Lieutenant William Calley was one of the most high-profile military trials in U.S. history. Calley was charged with the murder of 22 civilians during the massacre, although it is believed that the actual number of victims he was responsible for was much higher. The trial took place in 1971, and it was widely covered by the media. During the trial, Calley's defense argued that he was following orders from his superiors and that he had been acting under the stress of battle.

The prosecution, however, argued that Calley's actions went far beyond what was justified in combat and that he had engaged in deliberate and premeditated killings. The trial ultimately ended with Calley being convicted and sentenced to life in prison, but he was released on parole after serving just three and a half years.

While Calley was the only soldier to be prosecuted for the massacre, there was widespread criticism of the failure to hold other officers and military leaders accountable. Many believed that the events at My Lai were a result of broader systemic issues within the U.S. military, including the dehumanization of the enemy, the breakdown of discipline, and the failure of military leadership to intervene.

The massacre also had a profound impact on public opinion in the United States. It fueled the growing anti-war movement and further eroded support for the Vietnam War. The My Lai Massacre became a symbol of the brutality and moral collapse associated with the conflict and contributed to the widespread disillusionment with the war effort.

POLITICAL AND ETHICAL DIMENSIONS

The My Lai Massacre raised important ethical and political questions about the conduct of war and the responsibility of soldiers, officers, and governments in wartime. It highlighted the potential for individuals to commit atrocities when placed in an environment that encourages violence and dehumanizes the enemy. The massacre also raised questions about the accountability of military leaders, the role of military command in preventing such events, and the extent to which soldiers should be held responsible for their actions when following orders.

In the case of My Lai, the failure of military leadership to intervene and stop the massacre contributed to the scale of the atrocity. The actions of Lieutenant Calley and his men were not isolated, but rather the result of a broader culture of aggression, fear, and moral disengagement that existed within the military at the time.

Additionally, the My Lai Massacre exposed the limits of military justice and accountability. While Calley was convicted and sentenced, many felt that the punishment was insufficient and that the broader system of military command was not adequately held accountable for the massacre.

LEGACY AND IMPACT

The My Lai Massacre remains one of the most infamous incidents of the Vietnam War. Its legacy continues to shape discussions about war crimes, military ethics, and the treatment of civilians during armed conflict. The massacre highlighted the dangers of unchecked military power and the need for greater oversight and accountability in wartime.

In Vietnam, the My Lai Massacre remains a painful reminder of the brutality of the war and the suffering endured by civilians. For many Americans, it marked the end of the idealized image of the U.S. military and exposed the moral contradictions of the war.

The My Lai Massacre also served as a catalyst for changes in U.S. military policy and a reassessment of the conduct of war. It prompted debates about the rules of engagement, the protection of civilians, and the importance of ensuring that military forces are held accountable for their actions.

CONCLUSION

The My Lai Massacre was a tragic and shocking event that exposed the darkest aspects of the Vietnam War. It stands as a powerful reminder of the consequences of unchecked violence, the breakdown of moral principles in the heat of war, and the long-lasting scars left by such atrocities. The massacre also highlighted the need for greater accountability in the military and a more nuanced understanding of the complexities of war. As we continue to confront the challenges of modern warfare, the lessons of My Lai remain relevant in the ongoing struggle to ensure that the horrors of the past are not repeated.

CHAPTER 24
THE BHOPAL DISASTER
AN ACCIDENT WAITING TO HAPPEN

Union Carbide Plant

The Bhopal disaster, which took place on December 3, 1984, in the city of Bhopal, Madhya Pradesh, India, remains one of the worst industrial incidents in history. The disaster, caused by the release of a toxic gas from a pesticide plant, led to thousands of deaths, countless injuries, and long-term environmental damage. The Bhopal disaster became a tragic symbol of corporate negligence, poor safety standards, and the lack of accountability that often accompanies industrial operations in developing countries.

This chapter delves into the causes, consequences, legal implications, and ongoing legacy of the Bhopal disaster. The chapter is divided into several sections that explore the background of the Union Carbide plant, the technical aspects of the accident, the immediate aftermath, the long-term health and environmental effects, the legal and political consequences, and the broader implications for corporate responsibility and industrial safety.

THE UNION CARBIDE PLANT IN BHOPAL

Union Carbide India Limited (UCIL) was a subsidiary of Union Carbide Corporation (UCC), a large American multinational corporation. Union

Carbide had been involved in the production of chemicals and other industrial products for decades. UCIL operated in India, where the company established a pesticide plant in Bhopal in the early 1970s. The plant was designed to produce Sevin, a widely used pesticide, primarily for agricultural purposes. To manufacture Sevin, UCIL used methyl isocyanate (MIC), a highly toxic and volatile chemical.

MIC is a precursor in the production of Sevin, but it is extremely hazardous if mishandled. The dangers associated with MIC were well-known to chemical engineers and safety professionals; however, in the case of the Bhopal plant, safety standards and precautions were insufficiently addressed. The plant, which was located in a densely populated urban area, had inadequate infrastructure and lacked the robust safety protocols needed to prevent accidents.

The Process and Risks Involved

The process of producing MIC was a complex chemical reaction involving methylamine, phosgene, and water. These chemicals had to be handled with great care to avoid the production of dangerous byproducts. The Bhopal plant utilized large reactors to store and process MIC, which, under normal conditions, were supposed to maintain a temperature below 20°C. Any deviation from this temperature could lead to dangerous chemical reactions and the formation of highly toxic gases.

At the time of the disaster, the plant's safety systems were outdated, and there was insufficient maintenance and oversight. In addition to the technical risks associated with MIC, the company was also under pressure to increase production and reduce costs. To save on expenses, Union Carbide implemented cost-cutting measures that resulted in the reduction of staff, the shutting down of backup safety systems, and the failure to replace faulty equipment.

EVENTS LEADING TO THE DISASTER : THE MECHANICAL FAILURE

The disaster occurred in the early hours of December 3, 1984, when water inadvertently entered one of the MIC storage tanks at the plant. This was due to a series of failures in the plant's safety systems. A malfunctioning valve allowed the water to enter Tank 610, where the MIC was being stored. The water initiated an exothermic reaction, which led to a rapid increase in temperature and pressure inside the tank. The increase in pressure caused the release of toxic gases, including methyl isocyanate, hydrogen cyanide, and phosgene.

At the time of the incident, many of the plant's safety measures, including a large ventilation system designed to neutralize toxic gases, were not in operation. Workers were either unaware of the risks posed by the malfunction or were unable to respond effectively to the situation due to a lack of training and equipment. Within hours of the release, a massive cloud of toxic gas began to spread across Bhopal, affecting the densely populated areas surrounding the plant.

THE RELEASE OF TOXIC GAS

The release of MIC gas was catastrophic. The gas cloud spread across the city, exposing over 500,000 people to its toxic effects. The gas had a strong odor and caused immediate symptoms in those who inhaled it, including coughing, difficulty breathing, irritation of the eyes and throat, and nausea. The gas, particularly the methyl isocyanate, was so potent that even brief exposure led to severe respiratory distress.

As the gas cloud moved through Bhopal, it caused panic among the residents. People fled their homes in search of safety, but the gas spread rapidly, overwhelming the city's hospitals and emergency services. The local medical infrastructure was inadequate to handle the scale of the disaster, and many people died in the streets or at home before they could receive treatment. As the gas continued to spread, more people succumbed to its effects, and within hours, thousands were dead or severely injured.

THE IMMEDIATE AFTERMATH : CASUALTIES

The immediate death toll from the Bhopal disaster is estimated to be between 3,000 and 8,000 people. The majority of the victims were women, children, and the elderly, as they were more vulnerable to the toxic effects of the gas. Thousands of others suffered from severe respiratory issues, eye injuries, and poisoning. Many of the survivors were left with long-term health problems, including chronic respiratory diseases, neurological damage, and psychological trauma.

Hospitals were overwhelmed with victims suffering from the effects of the gas. Doctors and medical staff struggled to treat the large number of patients, as many of the symptoms were unfamiliar and the available treatment options were limited. International aid and medical teams arrived in Bhopal in the days following the disaster, but the immediate effects of the gas release had already caused irreparable damage.

THE DESTRUCTION OF HOMES AND INFRASTRUCTURE

The disaster also resulted in widespread destruction of homes and infrastructure. The toxic gas spread across a large part of Bhopal, and thousands of homes were damaged, either by the gas itself or by the subsequent panic and chaos. Many people were forced to abandon their homes, and entire neighborhoods were contaminated by the toxic chemicals released during the accident.

In addition to the immediate loss of life, the disaster left a significant number of people homeless and displaced. The lack of access to clean water, food, and medical supplies exacerbated the suffering of the survivors, many of whom had lost their livelihoods as well as their families and homes.

THE LONG-TERM EFFECTS : HEALTH CONSEQUENCES

In the years following the Bhopal disaster, the long-term health effects of the gas exposure became increasingly apparent. Many survivors developed chronic respiratory illnesses, such as asthma, bronchitis, and other lung diseases. The toxic gases released during the accident also caused severe damage to the nervous system, leading to neurological disorders in some survivors. Others developed eye problems, including blindness or partial blindness, as a result of the exposure.

The effects of the gas exposure were not limited to the immediate victims. Children born to survivors in the years following the disaster experienced a higher rate of birth defects, including mental retardation, physical deformities, and other congenital disabilities. The long-term impact of the disaster on the physical and psychological health of survivors has been devastating.

ENVIRONMENTAL DAMAGE

The environmental damage caused by the Bhopal disaster was equally severe. The toxic chemicals released from the plant not only affected the immediate vicinity of the disaster site but also contaminated the surrounding soil and groundwater. The chemicals used in the production of Sevin, including methyl isocyanate, were highly toxic and persisted in the environment for many years.

Efforts to clean up the contaminated site have been slow and inadequate. Decades later, the area surrounding the former Union Carbide plant remains highly contaminated, and many of the survivors continue to live in areas that are unsafe due to the presence of toxic chemicals in the soil and water.

LEGAL AND POLITICAL CONSEQUENCES

In the aftermath of the disaster, the Indian government faced intense pressure to hold Union Carbide accountable for the tragedy. A legal battle ensued, with survivors, environmental groups, and human rights organizations demanding justice for the victims. However, Union Carbide's response to the disaster was slow and dismissive. The company initially denied responsibility for the accident and argued that it was caused by human error or sabotage, rather than by any fault of the company's own design or maintenance practices.

In 1989, Union Carbide reached a controversial settlement with the Indian government, agreeing to pay $470 million in compensation to the victims. Many survivors and their families considered this settlement inadequate, as the amount was far less than the actual cost of the damage, medical care, and long-term health consequences. Critics argued that the settlement allowed the company to avoid full accountability for its role in the disaster.

THE LEGAL BATTLE AND WARREN ANDERSON'S ESCAPE

The legal response to the Bhopal disaster was also hindered by the lack of accountability from Union Carbide's leadership. Warren Anderson, the CEO of Union Carbide, was arrested in India following the disaster but was allowed to return to the United States before facing charges. Indian authorities were unable to extradite Anderson, and he was never brought to trial in connection with the disaster.

The failure to hold Union Carbide and its executives fully accountable for the Bhopal disaster remains one of the most controversial aspects of the legal response to the event. Survivors and activists continue to demand that the company's executives, including Anderson, be held responsible for their actions.

THE LEGACY OF THE BHOPAL DISASTER

The Bhopal disaster had a profound impact on the way the world views industrial safety, corporate responsibility, and environmental protection. The accident exposed the dangers of unregulated industrial operations and the failure of multinational corporations to adequately protect the communities in which they operate.

In the years following the disaster, there were significant changes to industrial safety regulations, both in India and around the world. Many countries, including the United States, adopted stricter regulations for the handling of hazardous chemicals and the safety standards for industrial plants. However, critics argue that much more needs to be done to prevent similar tragedies from occurring in the future.

ONGOING STRUGGLES FOR JUSTICE

The survivors of the Bhopal disaster continue to struggle for justice and accountability. Despite the passage of time, the victims and their families have not received adequate compensation, and many survivors continue to suffer from the long-term effects of the disaster. Environmental organizations, human rights groups, and survivors' organizations continue to advocate for the clean-up of the site, improved healthcare for the victims, and further legal action against Union Carbide and its executives.

The Bhopal disaster remains a stark reminder of the need for rigorous safety regulations, corporate accountability, and the protection of human rights in industrial operations. The struggle for justice continues to this day, and the survivors and activists fighting for their rights serve as a testament to the resilience of those who have been affected by the tragedy.

DID ANYONE GO TO JAIL FOR BHOPAL GAS TRAGEDY?

In June 2010, seven Indian nationals who were UCIL employees in 1984, including the former UCIL chairman Keshub Mahindra, were convicted in Bhopal of causing death by negligence and sentenced to two years' imprisonment and a fine of about $2,000 each, the maximum punishment allowed by Indian law.

CONCLUSION

The Bhopal disaster was a catastrophic event that claimed thousands of lives, caused long-term health and environmental damage, and exposed the failures of corporate responsibility, safety standards, and government oversight. The immediate impact of the disaster was devastating, and the long-term effects on the survivors and the environment have been equally severe.

The legacy of Bhopal is a cautionary tale about the dangers of industrial negligence and the importance of prioritizing human safety and environmental protection. Despite the passage of time, the survivors continue to fight for justice, and the world continues to grapple with the lessons of the disaster. The Bhopal tragedy remains one of the most significant industrial accidents in history, and its impact will be felt for generations to come.

CHAPTER 25
THE MADRID TRAIN BOMBINGS

The 2004 Madrid train bombings, also known as the 11-M attacks, were a series of coordinated terrorist bombings that took place on the morning of March 11, 2004, in Madrid, Spain. The bombings targeted four commuter trains during the busy morning rush hour, killing 191 people and injuring more than 2,000 others. The attacks shocked Spain, Europe, and the world, marking a grim chapter in the ongoing global fight against terrorism. The bombings, attributed to an Islamist extremist cell, were a devastating blow to Spain's sense of security and led to widespread political, social, and security consequences.

Train Wreckage At Bomb Site

BACKGROUND TO THE MADRID TRAIN BOMBINGS

Spain had long been considered a target for terrorist activity due to its involvement in the global fight against terrorism, particularly in its support of the United States following the 9/11 attacks. Spain's participation in the Iraq War, which began in 2003, was a significant factor that made it a target for terrorist groups such as Al-Qaeda. The decision of Prime Minister José María Aznar to support the U.S.-led invasion of Iraq was highly controversial in Spain, and it led to widespread protests throughout the country. The Iraq War became a focal point for radical Islamic groups who sought to retaliate against Spain for its perceived support of Western imperialism and its involvement in military operations in the Muslim world.

The city of Madrid, Spain's capital, had a population of over 3 million people and was a central hub for transportation, business, and culture. The commuter rail system in Madrid, known as the Cercanías, was one of the busiest in Europe, serving hundreds of thousands of people every day. The train system was seen as a vital part of the city's infrastructure and was heavily used during peak hours. With such a high volume of commuters traveling on the trains, the system was a prime target for terrorists seeking to cause mass casualties and draw attention to their cause.

While Spain had been a target for separatist terrorism from groups like the Basque separatist organization ETA (Euskadi Ta Askatasuna), the 11-M attacks were fundamentally different in that they were carried out by Islamist extremists with links to Al-Qaeda. The attacks were planned as a form of retaliation against Spain's foreign policy, particularly its involvement in the Iraq War.

TERRORISM IN EUROPE AND AL-QAEDA'S INFLUENCE

By 2004, Europe had become increasingly concerned about the spread of Islamist extremism. The Madrid train bombings were a stark reminder of the reach and threat posed by Al-Qaeda and its affiliates in Europe. Al-Qaeda, the jihadist group responsible for the September 11, 2001, attacks in the United States, had expanded its operations and influence in various regions of the world, including Europe. The group's ideology, which advocated for violent jihad against Western nations, had found fertile ground among radicalized Muslim communities across the continent.

Al-Qaeda's strategy was to carry out "spectacular" attacks that would inflict maximum damage and provoke widespread fear. These attacks were often designed to draw attention to the group's grievances against Western foreign policy, particularly in the Middle East, and to recruit more individuals to their cause. In the years leading up to the Madrid bombings, Al-Qaeda had been involved in a number of high-profile attacks, including the 2002 Bali bombings in Indonesia and the 2003 bombing of a U.S. military compound in Riyadh, Saudi Arabia. The Madrid bombings were a continuation of this global jihadist campaign, specifically targeting Spain as a symbolic response to its support of the U.S.-led invasion of Iraq.

THE ATTACK: EXECUTION AND TARGETING

On the morning of March 11, 2004, a series of bombs exploded on four commuter trains in Madrid, during the peak of the morning rush hour. The bombings occurred between 7:37 a.m. and 7:40 a.m., as the trains were on their way into the city center, filled with commuters heading to work or school. The attackers used explosives packed in backpacks, which were placed on the trains and detonated remotely. The four trains targeted were traveling on different lines of the Cercanías system, all converging near the Atocha train station, Madrid's busiest transportation hub.

The first explosion occurred on a train traveling from the suburb of Alcalá de Henares to Madrid's Atocha station. This train was carrying approximately 1,000 passengers at the time of the blast. The blast immediately killed 91 people and injured over 150 others. Within minutes, three more bombs went off on different trains, causing further carnage. The second explosion occurred on a train traveling from the nearby town of Leganés to Atocha, killing 43 people. The third and fourth explosions took place on trains traveling from the suburb of El Pozo del Tío Raimundo to the city center, resulting in 57 deaths and additional injuries.

In total, the bombings killed 191 people and wounded over 2,000 others. The attacks were among the deadliest in Europe since World War II, and the psychological impact on the population was immense. The bombings were highly coordinated, with the bombs timed to detonate almost simultaneously, ensuring maximum casualties and creating a sense of terror and chaos throughout the city.

The explosions were so powerful that they shattered windows and caused widespread damage to the trains and the surrounding infrastructure. The aftermath of the bombings was horrific, with the streets around the Atocha station filled with debris, bodies, and injured survivors. The chaos was compounded by the rush of emergency services, who struggled to manage the magnitude of the disaster. Hospitals were overwhelmed by the number of casualties, and the Spanish government declared a state of emergency to deal with the aftermath of the attack.

THE TACTICS AND METHODS OF THE ATTACKERS

The bombings were carried out with a high degree of sophistication, and the attackers used methods that were consistent with other Al-Qaeda-linked operations. The bombs were relatively simple but highly effective devices. They were made using explosives such as Goma-2, a powerful dynamite derivative, which was placed inside backpacks along with shrapnel to increase the destructive power of the blasts. The bombs were detonated using mobile phones, allowing the attackers to trigger the explosions remotely. The choice of mobile phone detonators was similar to other terrorist attacks carried out by Al-Qaeda affiliates in the past, providing a level of anonymity and control for the attackers.

The attackers also took advantage of the busy morning commuter rush, ensuring that the trains were filled with passengers. The precise targeting of trains in different parts of the city, all converging at the Atocha station, was part of the plan to maximize confusion and panic, making it difficult for authorities to respond in a coordinated manner.

The bombings were not only an attack on Spain but were also seen as a symbolic assault on the West. By targeting the Spanish government's political supporters and civilians, the attackers hoped to send a clear message to the international community about the cost of supporting U.S. military operations in the Middle East..

THE AFTERMATH: IMMEDIATE RESPONSE AND PANIC

In the immediate aftermath of the bombings, Madrid was thrown into chaos. Emergency services responded quickly to the scene, and hospitals were overwhelmed with victims. The Spanish authorities mobilized thousands of police officers, medical personnel, and emergency responders to help manage the disaster. Despite the best efforts of these teams, the sheer scale of the attack made it difficult to provide immediate care to all those in need.

Survivors of the bombing were in shock, many of them covered in blood or suffering from serious injuries. Many were trapped in the wreckage, and the aftermath was characterized by scenes of panic, confusion, and grief. Volunteers and locals rushed to help the injured, but the situation was dire. Madrid's public transport system, which had been paralyzed by the explosions, began to slowly return to normal as authorities worked to clear the wreckage and restore order.

The Spanish government quickly called for a national day of mourning and declared three days of official mourning, with flags flown at half-staff. The Spanish people were in shock, and many were left asking how such an atrocity could occur in their city. The attacks came just three days before the Spanish general elections, and this timing added a further layer of complexity to the political and social fallout of the tragedy.

PUBLIC AND POLITICAL REACTIONS

The reactions to the bombings were swift and intense, both within Spain and globally. In the immediate aftermath, there was widespread outrage and condemnation. Governments around the world expressed their solidarity with Spain, and leaders from all corners of the globe denounced the attacks as an act of terrorism. The international community recognized the Madrid bombings as part of the broader global war on terrorism, which had escalated in the wake of the September 11 attacks.

At the same time, the bombings led to a deep sense of fear and insecurity among the Spanish public. The sense of vulnerability was compounded by the fact that Spain had been seen as a relatively safe country from terrorist attacks, despite its involvement in the Iraq War. The fact that the bombings targeted civilians on public transport only heightened the feeling of insecurity. Many people in Spain began to question the government's security policies and the effectiveness of its counterterrorism measures.

The Spanish government, led by Prime Minister José María Aznar at the time, initially attributed the bombings to ETA, the Basque separatist group, which had been responsible for numerous acts of terrorism in Spainin the past. This initial assumption was based on the nature of the attack, as ETA had previously carried out bombings on public transportation in Madrid. However, within hours, investigators began to uncover evidence that suggested the involvement of Islamist extremist groups, and Al-Qaeda was quickly identified as the primary suspect.

THE POLITICAL FALLOUT: THE GENERAL ELECTIONS

The bombings occurred just days before the Spanish general elections, scheduled for March 14, 2004. The proximity of the attacks to the election created a volatile political situation, with political parties accusing each other of mishandling the response to the bombings. The ruling Popular Party (PP), led by Prime Minister Aznar, initially insisted that ETA was behind the attacks, despite mounting evidence to the contrary. This stance was seen by many as an attempt to avoid the political fallout that would result from acknowledging that an Islamist extremist group was responsible.

The opposition Socialist Party (PSOE), led by José Luis Rodríguez Zapatero, accused the government of attempting to manipulate the public's perception of the attacks for political gain. As new evidence emerged linking the bombings to Al-Qaeda, the PSOE gained ground in the election campaign, arguing that the government had failed to protect the country from the threat of terrorism.

In the days following the bombings, millions of Spaniards took to the streets in protest and mourning, and massive demonstrations were held throughout the country. Many Spanish citizens demanded answers about how the government had handled the situation and whether it had underestimated the threat of Islamic extremism. On March 14, just three days after the bombings, the Spanish general elections were held. The PSOE won the election in a stunning victory, and José Luis Rodríguez Zapatero became the new Prime Minister of Spain.

THE INVESTIGATION AND AFTERMATH

The investigation into the Madrid train bombings was extensive and complex. Within hours of the attacks, Spanish authorities began working closely with international partners, including the FBI, Europol, and intelligence agencies from other countries, to trace the origins of the bombings. In the immediate aftermath, dozens of suspects were arrested, and several key figures in the bombing plot were identified.

The investigation revealed that the bombings were carried out by a group of radical Islamists, some of whom were from North Africa and had ties to Al-Qaeda. The mastermind behind the attack was later identified as Abdelmajid Bouchar, a Moroccan national, and several other individuals, including fellow Moroccans and Spaniards, were arrested in connection with the bombings.

The investigators were able to trace the bomb-making materials back to a group of Islamic militants operating in Spain and Morocco. The attackers had used a network of safe houses, and the evidence showed that they had been planning the attack for several months. The group was linked to a larger network of Islamist extremists who were active in North Africa and Europe.

CONVICTIONS : CONVICTED DEFENDANTS

Jamal Zougam– guilty and given a 50,000-year jail sentence, was arrested two days after the March 2004 attacks.

José Emilio Suárez Trashorras- guilty and given between a 25,000 to 35,000-year jail sentence and was one of the first to be arrested

Hamid Ahmidan – found guilty and given between a 23- to 25-year sentence. Moroccan and a cousin of Jamal Ahmidan, these men took part in drug trafficking. His release date from prison is November 2030. After his release, he will be deported to Morocco.

Abdelmajid Bouchar – acquitted of all the bombings and still given between a 15- to 18-year sentence, was detained in Belgrade in August 2005 by Serbian officials. Released November 2023 and deported to Morocco.

Rachid Aglif – found guilty and given between a 15- to 18-year sentence. he was arrested in April and he was an alleged lieutenant of Jamal Ahmidan, who was suspected of having helped acquire the explosives. His release date is set for November 2025. He will be deported to Morocco. While a prisoner in El Castellón, he established a "special friendship" with imam Abdelbaki Es Satty, main suspect of the 2017 Barcelona attacks.

Youssef Belhadj – 30, acquitted of bombings but given 12.5-year sentence for membership of a terrorist organisation. He was arrested in Belgium in February 2005 by the Belgian Police, he allegedly set the date for the attacks and was in Spain for the last-minute preparations. Released November 2019 and deported to Morocco.

Hassan el-Haski – 45 acquitted of bombings but handed 12-year sentence for membership of a terrorist organisation. He was the leader of the Moroccan Islamic Combatant Group in Spain, which prosecutors blamed for the bombings. Haski, from Morocco, but having been "a long time resident of Molenbeek" Brussels), was arrested in the Canary Islands in December 2004. He was accused of having been aware of and having instigated the attacks. Released in November 2019 and deported to Morocco.

Mohamed Bouharrat, guilty and given 12-year sentence, was responsible for recruitment and gathering information on targets. Released in November 2019 and deported to Morocco.

Fouad el-Morabit, guilty, 12-year sentence was being held in March 2004 for allegedly belonging to the Madrid terror cell, he also had contacts with Rabei Osman. Released in November 2019 and deported to Morocco.

Mouhannad Almallah Dabas – guilty, 12-year sentence. Released and deported to Morocco.

Saed el-Harrak – guilty, 12-year sentence, currently described as an active cell member. Released in November 2019 and deported to Morocco.

Mohamed Larbi Ben Sellam, guilty, 12-year sentence, was allegedly in charge of bringing propaganda material to meetings of the cell. Prosecutors had asked for 27 years. Released in November 2019 and deported to Morocco.

Basel Ghalyoun – 26, guilty, 12-year sentence, was allegedly had links to Rabei Osman and the presumed ideological mastermind, Serhan Ben Abdelmajid Fakhet, a Tunisian who also died in the apartment blast. Prosecutors had sought a 12-year sentence. Released in November 2019 and deported to Morocco.

Rafa Zouhier – 27, guilty of obtaining explosives and given 10-year sentence. Released in November 2017 and deported.

Abdelilah el-Fadual el-Akil, guilty, nine-year sentence, was alleged close associate of Jamal Ahmidan, he had worked at a house on the outskirts of Madrid where some bombs had been made there. Prosecutors had asked for 12 years. Released and deported in November 2016.

Raúl González Peláez – guilty and given a 5-year sentence, was allegedly helped him gain access to the explosives in exchange for cocaine. Prosecutors had sought an eight-year sentence. Released in November 2012.

Sergio Alvarez Sánchez– guilty, 3-year sentence travelled in January 2004 to Madrid with a sports bag containing up to 15 kg (33 lbs) of explosives for Jamal Ahmidan. Prosecutors had sought a four-year sentence. Released in November 2010.

Antonio Iván Reis Palacio – guilty, given 3-year sentence, transported explosives to Madrid, Spain. Spanish prosecutors had sought a four-year jail term. Released in November 2010.

Nasreddine Bousbaa – guilty, 3-year sentence, he was allegedly helped forge fake documents. Spanish prosecutors had asked for 13 years in jail. Released in November 2010 and deported.

Mahmoud Slimane Aoun – guilty, 3-year sentence. he was allegedly trying to help Jamal Ahmidan forge documents. Spanish prosecutors had asked for 13 years in jail. Released in November 2010 and deported.

POLITICAL AND SOCIAL CONSEQUENCES

The aftermath of the Madrid bombings was marked by widespread grief, but also by significant political and social consequences. The bombings led to changes in Spain's domestic and foreign policies, particularly with respect to counterterrorism and its involvement in international military operations. Prime Minister José Luis Rodríguez Zapatero, who had campaigned on a platform of withdrawing Spanish troops from Iraq, fulfilled his promise and announced that Spanish forces would leave Iraq by May 2004.

The attacks also led to heightened security measures across Europe, with governments stepping up counterterrorism efforts and focusing on improving intelligence sharing and cooperation. The Madrid bombings were seen as a stark reminder of the ongoing threat posed by Islamic extremism and the need for vigilance in the fight against terrorism.

CONCLUSION: A DEFINING MOMENT IN THE FIGHT AGAINST TERRORISM

The 2004 Madrid train bombings were a defining moment in the global fight against terrorism. The attacks killed 191 people and injured over 2,000, and their far-reaching impact was felt not only in Spain but also throughout Europe and the world. The bombings were a brutal reminder of the vulnerability of democratic societies to terrorism, and they highlighted the complexity of the global struggle against jihadist extremism.

In the aftermath of the attacks, Spain's political landscape changed significantly, with the Socialist Party coming to power and withdrawing Spain's military presence in Iraq. The attacks also led to increased cooperation among European and international intelligence agencies, as well as a renewed focus on counterterrorism efforts worldwide.

The 11-M attacks will forever be remembered as a moment of collective trauma and loss for the Spanish people. They stand as a somber testament to the dangers of radicalization and the need for continued vigilance in the face of global terrorism.